The yesterdays of Grand Rapids

Belknap, Charles Eugene,
1846-1929. [from old catalog]

Nabu Public Domain Reprints:

You are holding a reproduction of an original work published before 1923 that is in the public domain in the United States of America, and possibly other countries. You may freely copy and distribute this work as no entity (individual or corporate) has a copyright on the body of the work. This book may contain prior copyright references, and library stamps (as most of these works were scanned from library copies). These have been scanned and retained as part of the historical artifact.

This book may have occasional imperfections such as missing or blurred pages, poor pictures, errant marks, etc. that were either part of the original artifact, or were introduced by the scanning process. We believe this work is culturally important, and despite the imperfections, have elected to bring it back into print as part of our continuing commitment to the preservation of printed works worldwide. We appreciate your understanding of the imperfections in the preservation process, and hope you enjoy this valuable book.

The YESTERDAYS of
GRAND RAPIDS

CHARLES E. BELKNAP

In Grand Rapids, Michigan
From 1854

First frame house in Grand Rapids, Erected 1833 by Joel Guild. Present location of the National City Bank

The YESTERDAYS of GRAND RAPIDS

By
CHARLES E. BELKNAP

GRAND RAPIDS
THE DEAN-HICKS COMPANY
1922

F574
.G7B4

COPYRIGHT, 1922
By CHARLES E. BELKNAP
Made in U.S.A.

With acknowledgment to The Grand Rapids Press, in which these articles appeared and from which they are reprinted by permission.

©ClA692856

Printed by
The Dean-Hicks Company
Grand Rapids, Michigan

Dedicated

To the Pioneers of Grand River Valley whose kindness and friendship have given me these priceless memories of a long and happy life.

PREFACE

This little book of retrospection is not in any way intended to be a complete history of Grand Rapids, although many historical events are recorded with strict adherance to the facts.

These "yesterday" stories are rather the personal memories of a man who has followed the trails of the Grand River Valley, by land and water, from the days when its splendid forest was the home of the Indian, to the present pagentry of our growing city with its commercial activities.

Through the days in which it has been my privilege to serve and share in this community's progress, my mind has received a class of impressions which the passing years have failed to efface, and in this book these memories are given without assumption or embellishment. I may not have done full justice to the noble men and women I have known, people who have left me with a love of my kind that even trial and misfortune has not dissipated. I may also be somewhat of a sinner in a literary way, yet if the stories are interesting and give pleasure, let them stand for all the apology that should be made and the author will be satisfied.

CHARLES E. BELKNAP

CONTENTS

	Page
At the Shipyard Forge	15
Why Men Came to Michigan	16
Indian Days	18
Shantytown and Wildcat Money	20
More Shantytown	22
The White Pine Canoe	24
The Pioneers' Winter Food	26
Recollections of Louis Campau	27
Louis Campau's Ways	29
Rix Robinson	30
"Governor" Stewart	33
Mr. Leitelt and the Telephone	34
Moses V. Aldrich	36
William Harrison	38
"Uncle Sam" Cooper	40
The Indian Mounds—I	41
Leveling the Indian Mounds—II	43
The Indian Plum Orchard	45
An Indian Wedding Tour	47
Indian Baskets	48
The Indian Trails	50
Where Did the Indian Go?	52
The Musk-e-Goes	54
A Day on the Olive Branch	56
The First River Steamboat	58
The Old River Fleet	59
A Honeymoon on a Raft	61
Early Council Days	63
Little Stories of Old Grab Corners	64
Grab Corners	66
Raising the Grade of Canal Street	67
Canal Street Jottings	69
Echoes of Old Dinner Bells	71
The National Hotel, the Site of the Morton House	73
The Burning of the National Hotel	74
The Public Well	76
The Fisk Lake Log Tavern	78
Fisk Lake and Pat McCool	80
The Site of Hotel Rowe	81
Shooting Under a Light on the Thornapple	83
Turkey Shooting	85
The Head and Tail of the Sturgeon	86
A Fish Supper with the Sons of Temperance	89
Winter Sports and Perils	90
The Bridge Street Toll Bridge	92
The First Garbage Collector	94
Kent County's Pioneer Jail	95
The First Sprinkling Wagon	96
The Police Patrol	98

	Page
Street Lights	100
Historic Railway Station	102
West Bridge Street, 1858 to 1891	104
Pearl Street Bridge	106
County Fair	108
The Old Arcade	111
Tramps, After the War	113
The First Railway Strike	115
An Old-Time Doctor	116
Surgery at the Shipyard Forge	118
The Sons of Malta	120
When Simeon Baldwin Killed the Bear	121
The Tale of Three Bears	122
Squire's Opera House and "Uncle Tom"	124
The First Strawberry Farm	125
The Shingle Maker	127
The Islands	129
The Mission Land	131
Rafting and the Chanty Men	133
Saddle Bag Swamp	135
The Wild Pigeon	137
The Straw Man	139
Pay Days	140
The Salt Water Baths	141
Colonel George Lee	143
Lieutenant Robert Wilson	145
Colonel Christofer W. Leffingwell and His Troop of Cavalry	147
The Annals of Fulton Street Park	149
Annals of Fulton Street Park—II	151
Annals of Fulton Street Park—III	153
Annals of Fulton Street Park—IV	155
The Elm Trees	156
The Blendon Hills	158
The Blendon Pines and Oaks	159
The Walnut Forest	161
The Black Hills	163
The River Rouge	164
Prospect Hill	167
Professor Edward W. Chesebro	168
The Stone Schoolhouse	170
Rev. James Ballard, Schoolmaster	172
The West Side Meeting House	174
With the City Firemen	176
Firemen of the Fifties	177
My Fire Service Before the Civil War	178
Experience of a Volunteer Fireman	180
The Volunteer Firemen of Early Days	182
Old Volunteer Firemen	183
Number Three's Engine House	186
Fire Company Number Three Visits Muskegon	187
General I. C. Smith's "Pony"	189
My Gray Fire Horse	191

The YESTERDAYS of GRAND RAPIDS

By Charles E. Belknap

At the Shipyard Forge

In the early fifties, when as a boy I came to the "faraway waters," forests covered the hills and valleys. In the windings of the river the steamboat passed between banks bordered with wild fruit trees, fragrant grape vines and meadows of wild flowers. In places the banks were blue with violets. Indian pinks were everywhere. It was an enchanted land from which came wild brooks, often bearing canoes loaded with native Americans.

Indians were not strangers to me, my father having lived all his life among the St. Regis tribe in the St. Lawrence river country. I sometimes think that I breathed into my system a lot of Indian spirits that float about in the maze of the autumn days. I would have willingly quit the river steamer for a seat in one of those canoes with its Ottawa paddler.

We came to Michigan because the government had given my grandfather a quarter-section of timber land as a reward for his services in the war of 1812. Father came to do the iron work on the boats being built in the shipyard located where the Pantlind hotel now stands.

By stage, river, canal, lake and railroad we arrived in Chicago, then known to the Indians as Chi-cog—"skunk water." In the getaway from this rightly named place we secured passage on a lumber schooner for Grand Haven, sleeping on the deck without blankets; then by steamer to Grand Rapids.

Until the white man came with a Bible in one hand but a jug of whisky in the other, the Indian was a pretty good fellow. When the smithshop was in order and the fires glowing with heavy forgings for the shipbuilder the Indian began to come in for gun repairs.

The first work my father did for one of them was a fish spear. With a grunt of approval he stepped into his canoe, went away upon the rapids and soon returned with a sturgeon long *as a rail* with which he paid his bill. North of the shipyard were sawmills, livery stables and Butterworth's foundry, whose factory bell was official time.

Canal Street north was a streak of black mud. On foggy days the wornout corduroy looked like alligators. Boys on adventure bound rolled up their trousers when going over.

The first business place south was Bentham's restaurant, then Daniel Ball's bank and beyond the tangle of streets afterward known as Grab Corners, a very proper term.

The shipyard forge soon became the roosting place for the loafers, traders, politicians, scandal peddlers and would-be statesmen. All territory south of Monroe-av. was "Shantytown," north of Monroe "Kent" and west side men were "Three B's". All stores were on the cash and carry plan. There not being many stores on the west side of the river every man going to work in the morning carried a bag, basket and bottle, the bottle for New Orleans molasses. The boys of these three sections seldom went abroad except in gangs. Because I lived on Waterloo and dad's shop was on Canal, I was neutral and had a chance to save my alley.

Why Men Came to Michigan

The financial panic of 1837 was a great disaster to the entire country and not until the Civil war did the money of the people find a solid foundation.

There had been a universal suspension of specie payments, the prices of foodstuffs had so advanced that bread riots were common in New England cities. Every young man with brain or ambition turned to the west for a home until it seemed all the people in the eastern states were moving. One of the early writers on the history of Michigan said that by 1837 it seemed all New England was coming to the state, every one singing the popular song—

"Come all ye Yankee farmers
Who wish to change your lot,
Who've spunk enough to travel
Beyond your native spot
And leave behind the village
Where pa and ma do stay.
Come follow me and settle in Michigania,
Yea—yea—yea—in Michigania."

There were four more verses to this siren song. The last verse promised, "We have first rate girls in Michigan."

This was misleading, for all the girls in the country not already promised were Indians not at all broken to white man's ways.

There were different trails leading to the new country. Those from Ohio to the southern end of Lake Michigan and by way of Detroit to the valley of the Grand were the most traveled. Thousands of young men with packs upon their backs and but a few dollars in their pockets left New England for a thousand-mile tramp into a wilderness. The girls remained at home until a cabin in the forest or a shelter in the village was made ready for them. Then they joined parties westward bound and came on either by trail, the river, the ox cart, or the primitive stage to join their mates. It was from such stock that Michigan was first populated and in the life of every one of these people was a story of privation, adventure and romance.

Eugene Carpenter of this city has in his home some of the woolen and linen spreads and sheets that his mother made during the seven years she was waiting for her lover to return from his farm in the woods to claim his bride in 1839. In use many years they are still serviceable. Money cannot buy these treasures of pioneer days.

My father used to tell us of a celebrated preacher in York State who tactfully complained to his diminishing congregation every Sunday that all the brain and muscle of the community was moving west and that only the cull timber was left. It seems to me now, after living here about all my life, that the valley of the Grand drew the cream of humanity from down east and that they were predestined to people our beautiful state.

Of course one did not expect a man to wade for days in the swamps of the Maumee or the marshes of the Kankakee without retaining a touch of malaria and we know many contracted the whisky habit, which they imparted to the Indian, by constant contact with shaking ague.

But in the nature of these early men was a wonderful brotherhood and desire to help the other fellow. When a farmer "butchered" it was the custom to send every neighbor a piece of meat, when the neighbor had a crick in his back all turned out and helped harvest his wheat or corn; when a man staked out a place for a cabin in the woods every one made a bee and in a day the heavy work was done. It seems as I look back that my father had an endless patience with and an excuse for every shiftless coot. To be sure I have seen him express it with the toe of his boot sometimes, but no one ever went away penniless or hungry.

The money of the thirties had been so valueless that men had little use for it. The love of it had disappeared from their minds and in its place had come a feeling for the other fellow and a resourcefulness and self-reliance. I reckon that is why every home volunteer of the Civil war was so proud and so secure when it was known that "Michigan is on guard tonight."

Indian Days

Until the late fifties all the Indians of this section of the state came to "the Rapids" to draw their payment from the government. They did not receive a large amount, but it was about all the good money that came into the country.

They came in the spring and bought their winter's trapping of furs and much fine basket and bead work. They put up their wigwams or tents on the islands in the river, and squaws heavily loaded, went about from house to house offering their merchandise for money or in exchange for salt pork, gaudy calico, or ribbon for their hair. They accepted all the food set before them, not expecting to pay for it, since they never thought of pay when they shared their often scanty supply. To an Indian business was one thing, hospitality another.

In physical appearance the Italian woman landing at Ellis Island is not unlike the early day Indian woman, but in artistic dress the squaw outshines her. The squaw's waist and skirt for dress-up occasions was usually blue broadcloth, skirt knee high, with leggings that fastened above the knee. Her clothing was ornamented with beads and porcupine quills. Smoke-tanned buckskin made her moccasins; and her long braids of black hair were dressed with bear's oil. She was not so attractive in her working garb and was often bowlegged and squatty from the heavy burdens carried upon her back. Not much could be expected of people who were strangers to soap and who moved to a new locality instead of trying to clean house.

My mother lived near Indians all her life and knew their ways of living. She had a place in her heart for the Indian mother. Often they came with pieces of cloth for her to cut into garments "same as the white squaw wore." One morning a big Indian stalked into the kitchen where mother was frying doughnuts. She motioned to the panful on the table and he ate about three dozen. "Heap good!" his only comment.

My mind is full of questions as I think of the Indian friends of my boyhood. Why did the government not send them clothing instead of money? Why did we send missionaries to the heathen when we had thousands of Americans in our own land needing help and salvation? Why did people gather in the pennies for the foreign missions and hold their noses in holy horror of the depraved Indian?

An Indian with his family came up the river one Sunday morning. Through the open windows of the barn-like church upon the bluff, came the hymn, "Praise God from Whom All Blessings Flow." The Indian, whose God created the O-wash-to-nong, leading a little fellow by the hand, his squaw following with a papoose upon her arm, came to one of the open windows. There were many vacant seats but they were not invited to enter. In the shade of the building the papoose slept in the arms of its sad-eyed mother. When the preaching, mostly of the fire and brimstone variety, was over, the hymns sung and the collection taken, the Indian helped his squaw into their canoe and they were soon lost in the swirl of the rapid river. Was that the reason that next day the wind picked up a heavy plank from a lumber pile and sent it like a thunderbolt through the gable of the main entrance of the church and out of the gable at the other end half way across the river? It must have been a hint to that congregation. They did not patch the scars for a long time and eventually this old church became a cooper shop.

Shantytown and Wildcat Money

From the first settlements at the Rapids in the early forties to the days of the Civil war that portion of the village south of Monroe-av. was known as Shantytown. Practically all of the travel up to 1858, when the Grand Trunk railroad came, was by stage over the plank road from Kalamazoo or by boat up and down the river. The steamer winding its way in the channels between the islands came to a landing at a barn-like yellow warehouse located at just about the present corner of Fulton-st. and Market-av. The wind south by west cleared away the lowland fog and from the upper deck of the steamer the passenger's first glimpse of Shantytown left him in doubt as to whether he was landing in Killarney or Montreal.

In the contest for freight the two-wheeled French dray was crowded by the green jaunting car of the Irish. There was one thing easy to learn in French and that was the cuss words, but in all the windings of Shantytown I never mastered the swear words of the Irish.

Because these dray men never understood what sort of names they were called, they never came to blows. Pierre going away with a barrel of molasses and Mike with a cask of corn whisky might collide, but there was that good fellowship that never hit a man after he was down, so the town prospered.

It was natural that Shantytown should grow, situated at the foot of the rapids where all boats were obliged to dock. People landing here found shelter and welcome at the Eagle hotel or the Rathbun house. There was keen competition between the two and their "runners" met the boats and shouted loudly the merits of their respective places. The Eagle had a darkey to black your boots. If they needed a shine just throw them outside your door and next morning they were ready for you. There were no bathrooms. If you needed a bath there was the whole east channel of the river at the back door and the water always clean.

The Rathbun in order to meet competition resulting from the bathing privileges, cleared away the tables in the dining room and had a dance every night. Also white sugar for tea and coffee, was served at the Sunday dinner.

Among the ebb and flow of people who came to these hotels were many men and women who stayed to build up the city and the state—men of the highest credit and industry who built machine shops, stores, warehouses, schools and fine dwellings. There might well be a bronze tablet at every corner of old Shantytown to mark the trail of both the Indian and the white man.

As I remember now Bentham's restaurant was to me the most important place in town. It stood where the Pantlind now stands and it may be the Pantlind's reputation for good things to eat is an inheritance rightly handed down. Bentham specialized in smoked venison. Sometimes he had boiled ham, venison stew with onions; in the winter oysters that came through in gallon wooden kegs; usually a kettle of pea soup to draw French trade, but dried venison always.

Nobody need go hungry, for if a fellow's credit was low he could set his traps for muskrat and trade the skins to Bentham for his daily bread. Ice cream had not been invented, but the present-day girl and boy has nothing over the boy who had a chunk of dried venison to gnaw on. Molasses candy was the great confection in those days, paid for with our big copper cents.

The floors and table tops at Bentham's were not scrubbed to excess, but all the same he liked the boys and the boys liked him. We watched him grow gray and when the Indians with canoe loads of bucks no longer came, the taste of the town changed to beer and pretzels and Bentham's became a thing of the past.

But of the time that I am writing the public could no more get along without Bentham's than they could without the Daniel Ball bank next door. This bank was open for business ten hours each day.

One never knew where the money was printed. Paper dollars changed value every time the sun went behind a cloud, just as eggs do nowadays.

Father had on his desk a weekly publication called the Bank Note Detector. When a customer paid his bill in paper money father consulted this authority to find how many cents on the dollar it was worth. Often a piece of fine picture paper was valued at ten cents on the dollar. This money was called "wildcat" and if a nervous person rocked the boat it sometimes became valuable as wall paper, being cheaper and more ornamental than whitewash. However, the Daniel Ball bank never became so demoralized.

It was reported that there was a nail keg of silver coin that kept traveling about the state by various methods in order to keep the paper money circulating. If by some mishap this coin got a day behind the bank inspector, it came to be my duty to take the gentleman out and keep him bass fishing until the emergency was over.

This explains why the cashier of the Daniel Ball bank, George Lee, who later became a captain and most valuable aid to Gen. Philip Sheridan, and I, were such close friends during the Civil war. Capt. Lee then befriended me in a hundred ways. I remember Capt. Lee telling the bank examiner that the Goddess of Liberty on the quarter-dollars was shivering with cold she had been pinched so often.

More Shantytown

All of Shantytown was sewered and graded long before the coming of Louis Campau. Grandville-av. was blazed first by a homesick cow that became lost in the woods. It skirted the shore of Sargeant's pond, crossed Snake creek on a log and disappeared over the hill. There were plenty of hills in Shantytown covered with grand trees, and creeks that wandered about and found their way to the river.

From the boys who sailed their toy boats on Sargeant's pond grew the men who fought in the river fleets of the Civil war. Today you could not locate the pond with an oil derrick, for the pond went up, not down. And from this pond was gathered the crew that rescued Mrs. Quirk's cow. A grand bit of water came out of a hillside, ran a short race and wasted itself in a swamp where the Union station now stands. Mrs. Quirk's cow had a fine pair of horns and they were the only part of the animal in sight above this swamp when the alarm was sounded.

The boys left the pond on the run, shirts and trousers were cast aside and into the mire they went. Clothes-lines were gathered from all the neighborhood and victory depended mostly on the staying quality of the animal's horns. If they had pulled off she would have been a total loss. But with clothesline and fence rail the cow was brought to dry land and it was a grand day, celebrated by all the neighbors on their way home from work. If it had not been for kind hearted helpers Mrs. Quirk's hospitality could not have lasted, but each helper had a little brown jug in reserve. For that locality, it was an event only equaled by the dedication of the present Union station.

Men were not envious in those days. If one built a house 16x20 the next fellow did the same. When there came the annual increase in the family a lean-to was added to the original structure. The census man had only to count the lean-tos to get the size of the family and study the clothes-line for the sex. In those early days all Mike had to do was carry brick to the top of a building and a man up there did all the work. When the bell on the foundry rang six o'clock he went home, smoked his pipe on the hillside and thanked God for the good place he had in the world.

In a vacant lot opposite the Eagle hotel the boys and girls of Shantytown staged a circus one summer. There was no lack of talent in the acrobatic work and the prettiest girl on Waterloo-st. gave a tight rope performance. For all that the circus went busted financially and had to give way to a man who put up a shingle mill. He was the inventor of a machine, run by steam power, that would shave shingles out of white pine blocks. That mill soon buried itself in shavings. It burned shavings for fuel and gave them away for kindling and yet they piled up. When the knives were not shaving, the whistle was blowing, for the smokestack kindled fires on all the roofs around about. Before many days the proprietor had skipped for Canada and the sheriff was in charge.

So within a short time the town lost two industries—a circus that started out to eclipse Dan Rice of national fame—and a monster that fairly devoured pine trees. But nothing could keep Shantytown from growing. Look at it as it stands today.

The White Pine Canoe

There are many old-time river men living in this vicinity who remember my painted canoe and at least one old deck-hand of the steamboat crew who threw stones in the fight with the thieving band of Indians that attempted to steal it away.

I had owned at different times several fine canoes and some common ones in which I picked up shingles and lumber from wrecked rafts and made good money for a young boy.

One year there came to the shipyard forge an Indian color maker with his squaw, who was an artist in bead work. Their camp was set on Island No. 2 in a grove of water maples.

They had a very large dugout canoe of beautiful lines which carried all their outfit, including an ugly dog to guard the wigwam. They were members of the Crane tribe at the Soo. The man mixed colors in an iron kettle over the forge fires and the woman sold her baskets and bead work to the ladies in Kent.

My father and mother were kind to them and when they went away the man said, "Twelve moons, come with canoe for boy." The next spring they came again and the man made me understand that there was a canoe hidden in the willows at Sand creek, the current in the river being too strong to tow it after his heavy dugout.

I found the canoe as directed. It was made from white pine, fancifully painted, and modeled after a Canadian birch bark. It was a beauty and I kept it in the basement of the shipyard forge except when in use on special occasions and never loaned it.

It was but a short time before it was taken out of the basement in the night and I began to search among the camps on the islands and found it with a lot of Indian canoes. I made a jump into it and started across the stream with several Indians after me.

The steamboat Michigan was just leaving the dock in the east channel and I sent my boat between the dock and the wheel, which was slowly turning.

The engineer shut off steam and the deck-hands began a free-for-all with their pond poles. Young Indian boys on the island began shooting arrows and the passengers abandoned the upper deck, and when the deck-hands could not reach the enemy with their poles they jumped ashore and began throwing stones.

My canoe was lifted on deck and the Michigan swung around in the channel and steamed away for the Haven. I was afraid to be set ashore at any down river point so remained on the boat, washing dishes to pay my freight.

On the way up next day we met the Indians coming down and Tom Robbins tried to run them down, but could not follow them into the marshes. They were just some of the riff-raff and the sheriff had ordered them away from the city, so my scalp was saved.

But I have only pleasant memories of the Crane and I love to think of him in some glen of the woods as he dreamed and worked over my canoe—a chip from the log here and there and then the color design intended to portray his vision of the white boy and the red man paddling a river that had no end—their friendship would never end. Of course he expected a gift in return and father gave him a five-tined spear made at the forge and mother made Gull, his squaw, happy with turkey red cotton for a dress.

When the Civil war came Crane qualified as a sharpshooter and his trail is lost in the swamps of Virginia.

THE YESTERDAYS

The Pioneers' Winter Food

One of the serious problems of the pioneer settler of any northern country is the storing of provisions for the winter months. Southern Michigan offered an abundance of game and wild fruit to the man who sought a home within its boundaries. Boys then, as now, had a great capacity for food and I remember my father's preparations for winter much better than I do my school lessons, and the cellar of our first home comes to mind more clearly than the parlor, for all its dulcimer, what-not, wax wreaths, and shell baskets.

This cellar had a dirt floor and riverstone walls. Along one side were the potato and apple bins; on the other the pork, beef, pickle and sauerkraut barrels and a bin for turnips, carrots and beets. Mother's spiced wild pigeons were a specialty and every fall father made an outing with others to Battle point down the river and put up barrels of black bass in salt. It was possible to get a twenty-five pound kit of salt whitefish at the Haven for two dollars. When it was time for Thanksgiving turkey we went over toward the John Ball Park country and shot one. And if we got two, mother made us give one to the minister.

This was long before the time of glass fruit jars or before one could buy canned stuff of any kind, but all during the summer we gathered the wild fruits, blackberries for jam, wild plums and verily the apple of temptation must have been the wild crabapple stewed down in maple syrup. During autumn days the kitchen was the drying place for pumpkins. A spokeshave was used to pare the rind, then they were sliced in rings and hung on a pole to dry. When well dried they were stored in the attic and rings were brought forth about once a week to be stewed for sauce or pies.

Apples, and peaches, when we could get them, were pared, quartered, strung on twine and hung to dry over the kitchen stove, where they made a fine place for flies to roost. Housewives who were finicky covered the stuff with netting.

Ham and shoulders—beef and venison—were dried in the old smokehouse. Then the cellar had its barrel of soft soap, kept well covered because for some reason or other it seemed always to be a trap for the family cat; and also its barrel of vinegar and cider. Beside them stood smaller kegs of wild grapejuice and elderberry wine.

Some families that had a member afflicted with shaking ague had a keg of wild cherries covered over with whisky. The mayor of the village added some of the inner bark of the cherry tree to his keg and one needed the appetite of a Georgia goober-grabber to share in his hospitality.

In some homes these fancy medicinal barrels fairly crowded the pork kegs and potato bins out of the cellar.

Nearly every family had its own chickens and the price of eggs did not go up every time the sun went behind a cloud; it also had a cow and had a pig. The pig ran at large and one year the village council found it necessary to pass an ordinance restraining people from emptying the dregs of their cherry whisky into the gutters.

Along about Christmas time jars of fresh lard, sausage and mincemeat were added to the cellar stock. Mince pies were made a dozen at a time and set out to freeze. Mother liked a bit of apple brandy added for flavor, but always had a temperance one or two laid by for the emergency of a guest who had signed "the pledge."

Thinking of those days brings to mind the peach blow potato that mother cooked in the steamer and brought to the table in its pink silk coat. A helping to a mealy mound of four with a generous covering of sausage sent a boy away to work with sunshine in his heart.

In spite of all the preparation a hard winter often found the provisions running low. Donation parties were given to help the poor, the sick or the needy. Charity was an individual not an institutional affair and it all came "out of the cellar."

Recollections of Louis Campau

I had as a boy—and still have—a great fondness for canoes. I had one that a white man made. Only when empty would it stay right side up. I kept this canoe to lend and nobody ever borrowed it the second time. But Mr. Campau, Uncle Louie, as we called him, helped me to buy a real one, an

THE YESTERDAYS

Indian dugout that sat on the water as well balanced as a duck and so light that one man might easily carry it over portage.

Uncle Louie had little confidence in canoes, but there came a time when he needed one in his business and so helped me pay for a good one. In the fall an Indian had received goods and money of Campau under contract to bring in return his trapping of furs and skins the following spring. However, he defaulted in payment—sold his pack to Bill Roberts in exchange for goods and skipped out for a sugar camp near Haire's landing down Grand River.

Campau started in pursuit with me for his paddler. On canoe voyages Uncle Louie always had a place in the bow with his shotgun across his knees. He made some very good shots, but much of the time he was singing little snatches of French song or pointing out interesting scenes and locations, talking much as an Indian would—bits of story or narrative. "At this place I once camped for a week," "here I tip me over and lose my gun," "there upon the high bank an old squaw had one bad fight with a bear. She take cubs out of log. Old bear come back sometime, strike with paw, squaw roll down bank, bear, too. In water squaw dive long way."

When we took this trip after the defaulting Indian we landed about ten miles below town. There were still patches of snow in the woods and we had no trouble in following a trail to the sugar camp. There were hand-made pine sap troughs under the many trees that had been tapped and near the fire, over which a large kettle of sap was boiling, was a large storage trough hewn out of a walnut tree. Nearby, an open front wigwam faced the fire, its floor strewn with cedar and balsam sprays.

The walnut trough was nearly full of sap. From there it was dipped into the kettle—and what interested me most was four little Indians having a hot bath in the contents. Stones heated about the fire had been dropped into the trough until the sap was of a very comfortable temperature. When the fire burned low a little Indian would hop out of the bath, pile more wood on the fire, add a hot stone or two to the bath and plunge into the sap again. I never had an appetite for Injun sugar after that trip.

But there was hard work as well as frolic in the sugar camp. Presently the Indian and his squaw came in from the bush with neckyokes on their shoulders and buckets of sap on either end. Uncle Louis marched up and demanded either the pay due him or the goods bought at Bill Roberts' store. To enforce his claim he gathered up the clothing belonging to the papoose in the bath. The squaw grabbed an ax and chased us out of camp. Uncle Louie left much of the clothing he had claimed scattered along the trail. I dropped the shotgun I had been carrying and my feet touched only the high spots so I reached the river bank a full half-mile ahead of my boss.

There was not much pleasure paddling against a strong current, but resting on my knees I did not miss a stroke, neither did I interrupt Mr. Campau, who expressed himself very clearly in a flow of French dialect until we made our landing at a dock back of the Eagle hotel.

Louis Campau's Ways

It was not difficult in the early days of the village to retain a memory of men's faces and to assign to nearly every man an occupation in the community.

In meeting a man there was time to size him up, class him as a farmer, a wood chopper, a doctor or a merchant; either a good fellow to touch elbows with or to give a cold shoulder. I must confess I sometimes made poor shots, but found first impressions usually good to build upon. It did not disturb my mind to find the man I had picked for a minister of the church around the corner, to be the engineer of the poker games on the steamer Olive Branch—broadcloth.

My recollections of Louie Campau are just those which any boy would have of a well known business man. I had sized up Mr. Campau as an Indian trader by the odor of his clothing. A person cannot handle muskrat, coon or smoke-tanned buckskin and not retain a bit of the Indian atmosphere. Moreover, Mr. Campau often wore articles of Indian clothing, buckskin coats, or in the woods or canoe beaded or quill-trimmed moccasins.

Most of the merchants or traders were content to buy the skins or furs brought to them, while Mr. Campau went out among the Indians soliciting their furs. It was always fair weather when good fellows got together and Mr. Campau was a good fellow. Nevertheless he had a shrewd weather eye and an anchor ready to throw—if his foot slipped he came down hard.

Mr. Campau could not have talked if his hands had been tied. When he had an interesting subject both hands and tongue were busy and if he lacked a desired word in English he substituted French or Indian.

My father often lunched with Mr. Campau in Bentham's restaurant. On one occasion Campau gave a dinner at Bentham's for a party of distinguished people from the east. The menu most likely was planked whitefish, roast wild duck, stew of venison ribs, French style, with dessert of wild honey, or wild crabapple sweetened with maple sugar and hot biscuit, washed down with sparkling apple cider fresh from the keg.

The Morning Enquirer was supposed to report the speeches made at this dinner, but at 3 a. m. no copy had been sent in. A. E. Gordon, the editor, was a guest at the dinner and my older brother, James, being compositor in charge of the edition, sent the office devil, a sleepy young brother, to ask him for the report. The young "devil" returned with a roast duck in his hand and said that Mr. Gordon was under the table hunting for his collar button and had told him to go back to the office and find out how a man was going to keep his shirt on when the collar button was gone.

Those capitalists went back east and reported Grand Rapids the best town west of the Alleghenies.

Rix Robinson

Rix Robinson was the first permanent white settler in Kent county. He came to the Thornapple river in 1821 and bought the trading post that had been established by the American Fur Co. and was managed by Mme. La Framboise. Afterward he established several other trading posts between the Thornapple and Grand Haven and during his life held many positions of trust.

I have a very clear memory of Rix Robinson and his wife. He came often to our shipyard forge and later to the west side shop. With my father I made one visit to his home near Ada on a spring morning about 1855.

We followed the trail that led through a land of wild flowers, dogwood, cherry, plum and crabapples. Indian pinks gave a blue haze to the ground.

My dog and I chased rabbits until dad had many times to whistle us back to the trail.

We passed several clearings where men were making homes and at each place were urged to "sit by." One tempting invitation came from a mother who said all she had was some fried chicken and hot biscuit. My dog sniffed and I winked at dad. That chicken sure smelled good. The mother was working salt into butter just out of the churn, and watching the oven where the baking was going on. And yet you hear of the hardships of pioneer days.

Arriving at Rix Robinson's we found the madam, who was a full-blood Ottawa Indian, working in the garden. She was so glad to see me that I was embarrassed. She sent me to the river with a pan of potatoes to wash and back the second time because I did not get them clean enough.

There was a cook stove, with the oven high up, at the end. The pipe ran into the chimney of the fireplace. The table of white pine had no linen. The tableware was in a homemade cupboard and I set the plates top side down with a steel knife and fork, and pewter spoon for each person.

Before the dinner was ready, a man, his wife and two boys landed in a skiff from up river. They had all their calamities in the boat and were moving to the Rapids, where work was plenty. When they had made a stake they expected to move back to the farm. Four more plates were set and we had a dinner of boiled potatoes, fried pork, gravy, bread, butter and milk.

In those spring days, the cows found leeks—wild onions—

so when you spread butter on your bread you had an onion sandwich. This was natural food for French and Indians. Others must cultivate an appetite for it. After the dinner had been eaten the mother of the boat party took from the waist of her dress some paper money and offered it in payment for the food. Mrs. Rix said: "Paper money no good—dinner good. Sometime I sit at your table. No come—other squaw come."

Many a family was helped along the trail by the wife of Rix Robinson. She was too big hearted to live within the fences of a city. The day we were at her home she wore white woman's dress. Her hair in two twisted braids coiled about her head was black as a raven's wing. I never saw her when there was not a bit of ribbon or a wild flower in her hair. The house was clean and tidy. On the beds were patch-work quilts of a design such as only an Indian woman could make. One could plainly see the Indian in everything.

I am not ready to say that there was anything striking about Rix Robinson. He was just a sturdy business man, very blunt and quick in his speech and positive in all he did. The Indians had great respect for him. He knew the value of money but it was not his god.

Rix Robinson was a part of the great out-of-doors. He had all the gifts of the white man but the eyes of an Indian, while Mrs. Rix had the eyes of the white woman and the soul of the Indian. Rix was an undeveloped naturalist. If he had put in print the things he carried in his head, the world would have profited as it has by the knowledge of Burroughs and Muir. He did not leave with us the printed word, but as the old residents follow the trail to the east, those who have good eyes can see in the haze of years, the figure of a Che-mo-ka-man—a white man good to look at, to hail as a fellow well met, a sample of courageous men who went forth to conquer the wilderness.

In a river bottom field below the village of Ada, there is but the ghost—a few of the stones—that made the foundation of his cabin which sheltered rich and poor, young and old, as they made their journey down the river to the Rapids. A monument at the top of the hill in the cemetery marks Rix Robinson's grave, but it does not end his story, because we have for all time his trail—now Robinson-rd.

"Governor" Stewart

In recent years the crowing of a candidate for governor from every hilltop in the state has reminded me that in 1856 Grand Rapids had a volunteer who seemed inspired to devote his life and fortune as well as his two hundred and eighty pounds of avoirdupois to restoring prosperity to an afflicted people.

The national issues were buried beneath state and local affairs and politicians often spat on their hands and those who had coats pulled them off and argued the questions in the middle of the road. Some contended that money was tight; others that it was loose, but that all the men on Canal-st. were tight.

The ship forge and yard, at the foot of Lyon-st. were the busiest places in town. Men gathered in the shop to discuss politics and often dad would threaten to throw them out into the basin with the driftwood they so interfered with the work.

Then along came a candidate for governor, a stranger in our midst. He registered at the Bridge-st. hotel as the Hon. William Stewart, wore a plug hat and a long-tailed coat and hired a boy to scatter handbills announcing a public meeting when he would lay before the people his plan whereby to save the country.

Bill Stewart, as he was soon called, found his way to the forge. He chewed navy plug tobacco and when clinching an argument the overflow from his mouth was as good as the moral of a dime novel to the young tobacco aspirants. He really made himself Grand Rapids' candidate for governor and it is to be regretted that he was not nominated. His portrait would have made history in the halls of fame.

From the day of his arrival Stewart and Louie Campau were at war. There was a seat by the side of an anvil, a punch block, that the Hon. Bill appropriated much to the smith's disgust, for it had been Uncle Louis' place. Finally, a Saturday came when there was to be a torchlight parade, after which at a bonfire in front of the Rathbun House in the evening, Hon. Bill would talk.

The smith finished a bull ring for the steamboat under construction in the yard and threw it on the cinder pit red hot just as the governor, as we had learned to call him, came puffing in the front door. Uncle Louie was on hand and with a pair of tongs placed the hot ring on the punch block, where the big man at once sat down. Not being trained to quick movements his hide had lost its commercial value by the time he reached the shipyard basin. Uncle Louie was more speedy in leaving by the front door.

There were several of us boys tinkering guns and fish spears in one corner. I couldn't remember what became of Stewart and so the other day I asked one of those boys, now a great-granddad of the town, if he remembered. He declares that the Hon. Bill left town face down on a lumber raft.

In all the days since 1856, if Grand Rapids has had a candidate for governor, some joker has placed a bull ring to trap him. Mud slinging is nothing like as effectual as a hot iron.

Mr. Leitelt and the Telephone

One day in the late fifties I wandered into the forge of the McCray Bros. machine shop, then on the bank of the east channel of the river below the Eagle hotel.

The two young Leitelt brothers were forging a heavy piece of iron, such as only strong men could handle. It was not the hot metal that attracted me, for I was familiar with forgings from my first days. It was the two brothers. I doubt if there were two other men in the town of such fine and powerful physique. Adolph guided the blows, his brother behind the anvil swinging the sledge. It was toward night and the heated metal and the glow of the charcoal fires lighted the building, casting deep shadows all about.

I had been reading the tales of Vulcan, "God of Fire," which my mother termed mythical, but here was Vulcan in action; bared chest and arms, muscled and coated with hair; giants midst the flakes of fire. When the heat worked off the forging was returned to the fire, more coal heaped on and with man at the bellows the anvil was soon ringing to the blows. Many passers dropped in, for the scene charmed men as well as boys.

It was thus Big Adolph Leitelt came into my life and for many years was associated in my mind with the forge, though he served in many capacities. In 1870 he was a city councilman and chairman of the fire department committee. I was the foreman of the very busy No. 3 company, for this was just about the time of lumber yards, sawmills, and stove-heated dry kilns, and the town fairly oozed with pitch, pine, shavings and sawdust.

The possibilities of the telephone were just coming to light —a few believed but nearly every one scoffed and ridiculed the idea of talking by wire.

William Hovey and his able assistant, Mr. Apted, were heads of the Grand Rapids Plaster Co. Mr. Hovey's office on Monroe-av. and Mr. Apted's at the mills three miles away were the first places connected by wire. This was an experiment and was made largely with a view of securing quick fire service.

I was eagerly watching the venture. One day Mr. Hovey sent his buggy for me and on the way picked up Mr. Leitelt. We entered the office to find several other men there. Mr. Hovey said to the alderman: "Apted at the mills wishes to talk with you." He placed the receiver to Mr. Leitelt's ear and told him to speak up loud. Leitelt's voice was in proportion to his body and when he spoke everything in the office vibrated. Mr. Apted replied with a joke that caused a roar of laughter.

Mr. Leitelt dropped the receiver, going out into the hallway. It was empty, so he explored the coatroom and every place where a man might be concealed, all the time getting more impatient until at last he turned on Hovey with a roar that was far from a song of peace and returned to his own office in full belief that he was being made the victim of a farce.

The evening after, Mr. Apted cornered Mr. Leitelt in Leppig's coffee house in the Arcade.

Leppig's coffee was the best ever and gave men confidence to meet the whirl of new events. Mr. Leitelt thereafter became a power in the common council for the fire department. His assistance was certainly needed for insurance rates had gone sky high and much equipment was needed to keep up with the growth of the city. These primitive telephones were installed in some of the engine houses, as was also the fire alarm box system. The number of persons who took stock in the innovations was limited, but nevertheless it was the initial step toward our present fine system. About the time these improvements were being made Gen. I. C. Smith was appointed chief of the department and I was advanced to the position of assistant chief.

Fire department days did not close my association with Mr. Leitelt. In 1884 we were the targets for the public to shoot at—the victim to fill the office of mayor at one dollar per annum. I beat him to it, for size was of no advantage when it was running that won.

But after all the years Mr. Leitelt comes more often to memory with the glow of the forge, the ring of the anvil, the swing of the sledge. I am convinced boyhood memories are the more lasting.

Moses V. Aldrich

One snowy day years ago I was buying a pair of shoes in the Cole brothers' store on Monroe street when Mr. Aldrich came in followed by an old woman. He said to Mr. Cole: "Fit this woman to a good pair of shoes; if her stockings are wet get a dry pair. Send the bill to the office."

Said Mr. Cole to me: "Moses Aldrich is the best customer we have. I don't know where he finds the old people that follow him in here."

I had respected Mr. Aldrich a long time as banker and business man—but this incident gave me a different slant at his way of doing things. For years he gave his valuable time and out of pure kindness of heart served as county superintendent of the poor and carried the burden of the county farm upon his shoulders, lifting it out of the opprobrium of "poorhouse," a term so terrifying to unfortunate people. When the township supervisors could not be made to understand the need of funds Mr. Aldrich put his own pocketbook on the counter.

He did not believe that mush and skim milk could take the place of beef and cabbage on the table before men who needed good, hearty food. He said to one housekeeper, "This man needs food, not curses."

Mr. Aldrich earned a lot of money and always shared with those who were unfortunate, but he was the happiest on circus day when his funds passed the barefoot boys of the street into the big tent and furnished endless rounds of lemonade and peanuts for the gang.

Before the Civil war wild money queered the country; then during and after the war government paper money fell below the water line and gold and silver disappeared. Money panics followed each other so closely they often collided. Men could not finance any kind of an enterprise. Many, in order to pay their workmen, issued their own shinplasters and small tokens redeemable in sums of five dollars. Then came a time when the government issued gold notes of ten and twenty-dollar denominations and for some years a discount of twenty per cent or more was required on paper money.

The gold coin note was yellow to distinguish it from the greenback. Timid people hoarded the gold notes and the term, "Yellow-legged bankers," was quite commonly applied to wealthy widows. Gold notes circulated but were out of sight most of the time.

It seemed every banker as well as politician in the country had a plan to resume specie payments. The bank of Ledyard & Aldrich was on the corner of Monroe and Ottawa. One day there appeared in its window a brass-hooped barrel full of gold eagles, lying on its side, the head removed and its contents displayed to the delighted gaze of the people on the street.

Mr. Aldrich announced that "the way to resume is to resume," the first banker in the United States to start the game. Gold, silver and yellow-legged gold notes came out of hiding and the much abused greenback was placed at par. Shinplasters and brass tokens disappeared along with fish-scale three-cent coins and Canadian twenty-cent quarters.

Out of Wall street came a wail of dismay at the thought of

losing their exorbitant discounts and personal calls from its magnates were made on the banker of the lumber town.

If Moses Aldrich had not been so modest he might have become the national secretary of the treasury. Mr. Aldrich was mayor of the town in 1868-69-70. He was not long with us, but every day of his fifty years was a benefit to the town.

William Harrison

Seeing an occasional old farm wagon about the country with the name Harrison on the side, has prompted the writing of a few words regarding an early time industry—the Harrison wagon works, and its interesting founder.

When Mr. Harrison, in 1856, came to Grand Rapids from Kalamazoo, where he first began the manufacture of farm wagons, he built the stone fort, as it was called, upon the river bank on Front-st., near Third, which for many years was headquarters for the Harrison wagon. This was the first building on the river in that vicinity. The canal had not been built and a deep basement allowed for the blacksmith shop, the main floor a woodworking room and the second floor a paint shop, with a rope tackle block by way of elevator.

Equal to the coming of a circus was the arrival of the wagon train, which came over the plank road from Kalamazoo, loaded with material and machinery for the Front-st. shops. The railroad had not reached the town and all the freight came by the river or over the ungraded highways.

Wagons were in great demand and every part of them had to be made by hand. They required good material and skill in making. The locality had an abundance of fine timber, but it was standing in the forest and had to be cut and well seasoned before it was fit for use.

One of the first transactions of Mr. Harrison was the purchase of the seasoned oak plank flooring from the barn of Haines Edison and the oak fence rails inclosing the farm, which material was bucked up into lengths and shaved into spokes and felloe stock. Mr. Edison received in payment the first farm wagon made in the Harrison works.

The buyers of farm wagons had very little ready money

and needed long-time credit, so the financing of the factory was a far greater problem than that of building the wagon. For years wagons were exchanged for lumber or anything the farmer raised. The produce of the grower paid the wages of the men, but the iron, paints and oils were bought in outside markets and had to be paid for in money.

Mr. Harrison's motto was "More wagons." His every effort was to produce more wagons than any other factory in the world. Only the Studebaker factory at South Bend turned out a greater number. Soon after the Civil war the government backed the South Bend company in order that the great west might have transportation. Mr. Harrison had no backing other than the local bankers could give with long-term farmers' notes as security. At one time Mr. Harrison had in his office an apple barrel full of notes tied in alphabetical bundles.

But the factory under competent management spread from the old stone fort to many branches, sawmills, smith shops, vast lumber yards. The manufacture of wagons became a leading industry of the north; other factories sprung up and competition was fierce, but still more wagons was the Harrison slogan, backed up with bulldog persistency. For years long trails of wagons were a common sight on Monroe and Canal-sts., the Harrison name going to every part of the world.

In later years Mr. Harrison lived on the crest of West Bridge-st. hill, his great plant was moved to the north end of the west side and he drove between home and factory in an open buckboard wagon. He was very simple in his taste. His lunch at noon often consisted of bread with a thick-cut steak toasted on the end of an iron rod over the coals of the battery boilers, the grimy stokers and greasy engineers sitting about with their full dinner pails, enjoyed their noon-day meal no more than did the "old man."

He never spent an idle day and at one time was very well-to-do, but unfortunate investments in oak forests that turned out to be huckleberry marshes depleted his resources and he departed this life just about the time a black frost in the guise

THE YESTERDAYS

of a gasoline smudge from the newly-invented automobile settled upon the wagon industry.

"Uncle Sam" Cooper

With permission I quote from the South Bend Times-News of a late date:

"Uncle Sam, the one and original, has made his debut in South Bend in the person of W. E. Cooper of Pittsburgh, Pa. 'It's all because of my whiskers,' said Mr. Cooper, who has seen seventy-nine years, and has been called upon many times during the past quarter of a century to act as the famous American 'uncle'.

" 'I don't use paint or powder or other fixin's, except my suit and hat—that's why they call me the only original Uncle Sam. It started back in Pittsburgh about thirty years ago when the folks began to call me that and since then I have been kept pretty busy dressing up for special occasions.

" 'During the war I did what I could to help along the sale of thrift stamps and served in all the four Liberty bond drives. I guess I have been in nearly every state in the Union attending conventions and celebrations of various kinds. It's a great life.' "

People might be interested to know that Mr. Cooper was formerly a resident of Grand Rapids. In 1880 he established a commercial collection agency in the Ledyard, now the Kelsey block, on Ottawa-st., employing ten clerks. Among the men with whom he did business and whom he remembers well were Allen Durfee, E. S. Pierce, Morgan and Avery, H. W. Green, monument dealer; Dr. Robinson, dentist; Shellman, the optician and A. B. Knowlson. During Home-coming week in the year of 1890 Mr. Cooper represented Uncle Sam for the A. B. Knowlson Co. in the street carnival held at that time, attracting a great deal of attention. Mr. Cooper was also one of the organizers of the Grand Rapids Humane society. When the basement of the Widdicomb building was being excavated Mr. Cooper, Dr. Maxim and Rev. Charles Fluhrer, the beloved pastor of All Souls' church, who happened to be watching the work, were much shocked at the abuse of the horses by their drivers. It was the finishing touch to much agitation along this line and the society was formed with Rev. Fluhrer as president and Dr. Maxim as secretary, and Mr. Cooper was chosen special deputy sheriff and sent to Chicago to study the operations of the Humane society in that city. Mr. Cooper made enemies, for the work led to court where cruelty to animal cases were often bitterly contested.

For ten years all the time he could spare from his other interests was devoted to humane work with no financial return for his services.

In the strenuous days of the recent World war Mr. Cooper came to his old home town and led the Liberty bond parade, marching at the head of the column as Uncle Sam, but few of the thousands looking on knew his history.

He is now a resident of the Elks' Home at Bedford City, Va. In spite of his failing eyesight he is able to find his way around and is willing to don his striped trousers and stovepipe hat to oblige his friends.

Mr. Cooper's mortal days may have an ending but the wit and wisdom of the cartoonist will keep Uncle Sam on the front page as a type of the great American.

The Indian Mounds—I

Who were the mound builders of western Michigan is a question that has often been asked but never fully answered.

The works of the mound builders were found all over eastern America. Although simple in form they convey by their contents and structure more in regard to the habits and art of their authors than can be learned from all their other works combined.

The burial mounds and their contents tell us of individual traits, something of the social life, their tastes, and something also of the diseases to which they were subject.

In 1874 a committee consisting of Edwin A. Strong, Capt. W. L. Coffinberry and Dr. Joel C. Parker explored many of the forty-seven mounds then remaining in and about the Rapids. These mounds varied from three to fifteen feet in altitude and in diameter from ten to more than one hundred feet.

THE YESTERDAYS

Early missionaries and traders said the Indians of their day had no knowledge of the origin of these mounds. They only knew they were the work of men and had great veneration for them.

On the mission land along the river south of what is now Bridge-st. stood many of these mounds, which were leveled in the grading of streets in the fifties. For several summers I was water boy for the men who did this grading and had ample opportunity to gather the flint arrowheads and other implements that were unearthed in nearly every burial mound along with the bones of the vanished race.

There were three very ancient mounds at the present corner of Allen and Court-sts. In one of them was a stacked mass two feet in diameter and twenty inches high of jet black flints and arrowheads of the finest workmanship. No flint of this kind was found in any other mound. Below the original surface of the ground was found a strata of human remains and with these bones were earthen vases, pieces of clay pottery, bears' teeth with holes drilled for stringing as ornaments and many stone smoking pipes of fine design.

In digging a sewer trench a few years later two nuggets of pure silver weighing thirteen pounds and one flake of copper weighing fourteen pounds, were found. These, with a great accumulation of other curiosities, were sent to the Peabody Museum in Massachusetts and the Smithsonian Institute in Washington.

Alfred Preusser, the jeweler, bought from me quite a bit of silver ornament that I had collected, which he melted to use in his shop work, neither of us realizing its historic value at the time. By the time of the Civil war I had accumulated so many relics from the mounds that the attic of our home was full of skulls with grinning teeth, arrowheads, bits of pottery, smoking pipes of clay, and stone implements.

This stuff, with the paddles I had used in my canoes, the bead work moccasins and snowshoes—souvenirs of many an Indian's good will—went up in the smoke one windy night. If there is a relic of this collection left it is well covered by the walls of the Star mills south of Bridge-st., for our home was located there on the bank of the river at the time I was called to war.

Every state has had its students of the mound builders and among the most interested here, I had personal acquaintance with Capt. W. L. Coffinberry, Dr. Joel C. Parker, Dr. William H. DeCamp and Thomas Porter.

The Civil war called Coffinberry and DeCamp to service in the army. Every one of these men would have been a treasure if paid a salary and kept in the state's historical service. They did leave traces of their work in many of the museums of the country, but in their days there were no stenographers and no funds provided for this exploration. These men followed the laborers who leveled the mounds and frequently found use for a boy who should have been in the old stone schoolhouse, but who found ancient history more satisfactory if studied on the ground.

When Capt. Coffinberry unearthed a skull Dr. DeCamp explained how old its owner must have been. Dr. Parker judged by the teeth, the kind of food he lived on, and Mr. Porter by the contour how much brain power he had developed. Having the last word I put the trophy in the wagon and so the group worked in harmony.

Leveling the Indian Mounds—II

When there was no longer use for the Mission land on the west side, it was sold by the government to eastern parties who platted it for residential and commercial purposes, with no regard for its scenic beauty.

It was a project of cutting down or filling up, and so the Indian mounds, with their historic contents, were carted away to fill the low places.

There was no regret over this leveling of the mounds. Even the men who gathered the curios reaped considerable financial benefit from their sales to museums.

There was little real money in circulation and the silver coins that came from Boston to meet the pay-rolls for the labor was appreciated by the business interests of the city.

This work, which gave employment to many men, was directed by two brothers, Boston men—William Hovey, a fairly tall man, and Albert Hovey, a very small one, whom the employed men tagged "Little Britches." He was very popular on pay day.

There was no school in the summer and the writer had the job of carrying drinking water to the various gangs of workmen. Microbes had not yet arrived in the valley, so there was but one water pail and one long-handled dipper from which every one drank.

The first laborers were Irish. One hardly need read the pay-roll to discover this for they kissed the "Blarney Stone" every day, they talked and sang, and every Saturday night a Donnybrook fair was held along Canal-st.

Two-wheeled dump carts, wheelbarrows, picks and shovels, made up the contractors' outfit. A short clay pipe and an iron tobacco box filled every morning, with a bit of fresh punk in one corner, constituted Pat's kit.

Arrived on the ground, Pat sat down, filled his pipe, took from the punk a bit, that with a puff of breath became a live coal, dropped it into the pipe and with a long-drawn sigh filled his mouth with smoke. Then the lighted pipe "passed the loan of a fire," and all the gang spit on their hands and the dirt began to fly.

These men enjoyed their work. With pipe stem clinched between the teeth, they sang through their nostrils in a way to charm bumble-bees out of their nests in the grass.

Half the first summer passed before they began to level the grounds on the spot where the Powers & Walker factory now stands and fill in Front-st. to the north.

These mounds must have been a resting place for many killed in a battle. Entire cart-loads of grinning skulls and ancient bones came to light and these were too much for the nerves. Pat quit the job and never came back and with him went the melodies that had come from overseas in the steerage.

It happened about that time that all Holland seemed to be climbing over the dykes and the leveling of the mounds continued, but under a different dialect.

The Dutch had about the same tobacco boxes, but each

one carried a flint and steel with which, by patient practice they could get a light but they never lost more than ten minutes in starting a smoke. These men wore wooden shoes and corduroy trap-door trousers.

They might have remained at work had not some boys—Richard Blumrich could name them—gathered the bleached bones of a horse and assembled them about a stump on the trail to Gunnison swamp, near where some of the men were living. The ghost standing in the moonlight was one bone too many.

It was coming winter and the grading was laid by for the season. The tide of settlement drifted for a time to other parts of the town, but many fine homes were built on the Mission land, which finally has become a network of railways and busy factories.

There were forty-six mounds all told on the Mission land. One long, flat-topped ceremonial place was on the river bank at the present western terminal of the Pere Marquette railroad bridge.

Tradition says the Pottawatomies, who came here as the friends of the Ottawas, were the people of the fires. They banked in earthen pots, fire that was never permitted to die out. A fire always burned on this mound up to about 1840. When it was carted away to fill a place in a street I watched the diggers for days, hoping to find something of interest to my good friend Capt. Coffinberry, but aside from clamshells, ashes and charcoal, it contained little of value. Scattered bones of animals that were found well toward the bottom, were thought by some to be the bones of a mastodon.

At the east end of the Lake Shore railroad bridge there is a group of Indian mounds still standing. They were partially explored on several occasions and the relics of very ancient origin taken from them. Some of these treasures are in our Kent museum and others in the Smithsonian at Washington, D. C.

The Indian Plum Orchard

Not until the early seventies did the last trace of the Indian plum orchard, on the west side of the river below the present site of the Wealthy street bridge, disappear. Then it was slashed into log heaps with other bottom land trees and burned in order to make pasture.

This orchard was well known to early day people. Plums grew in profusion on river bottom lands—but these red, yellow and blue plum trees were in circles about a moss-grown basin of about two hundred feet. It was believed to be an assembly place for Indian ceremonials; very early white men told of corn dances held there.

I do not know who cleared away the orchard. My memory is of the wonderful training place its moss-grown ring made for young acrobats and of delicious plums and wild grapes which we carried away by the basketful for our mothers' winter supply of preserves.

Then the crabapple, a sociable little tree, had grown up in any vacant spot, not particular about location; in the spring its pink blossoms grew so thick that they crowded each other off the branches. If a boy tore a hole in his trousers the tree furnished thorns to mend the tear. The man who named this fruit had never tasted the jam that mother made with maple sugar and set away in jars in the cellar or he would have found a better name for it than "crab."

When I first played there in the fifties, there was under a dense growth of vines, a driftwood wigwam with a hole in the peak to let out the smoke. A pole bed with swamp grass, fit only for a homeless dog, occupied one side.

One day there came to our home on Waterloo, now Market street, an Indian woman with baskets to trade for food. She told my mother that her daughter with a newly-born babe was lying very sick in the plum orchard wigwam.

Mother, in company with a French woman who lived near Sargeant's pond, took a basket of food and went with the squaw in her canoe.

The French woman brought the little pappoose back with her. Her own house was so full of children that her old man slept in the stable, but other nearby mothers gave baby clothes and furnished catnip tea and Van, the milkman, left an extra dipper of milk every morning.

That little pappoose had lullabys in Irish, French and English and if it had stayed until it had learned to talk the dialect of the neighborhood its Indian mother would have disowned it. But one day when the mothers were having a quilting bee she came and carried it away, strapped in a blanket to her back.

Leading to and from the plum orchard were well worn trails to the hills on the west and up and down the river banks. The Black hills across the river, the council pine up the stream, may have been the guide to the orchard, but just what was the Indian belief or mystery of this place or why the trees were planted in circles of red, blue and yellow, will probably never be known by the white man, but it must have been common ground to the Indians for long years before the first white settler came to the valley.

There was no evidence that it was a ceremonial place, although it was within half a mile of the Indian mounds.

An Indian Wedding Tour

One early spring day there came up the river a Mackinaw boat with a crew of four—two young Indian couple—upon a wedding tour which, as the custom was those days, would continue until the ice closed the lakes to navigation.

They brought a message to my father from an Indian friend, and also wanted to trade some moccasins for a spear, which would have to be forged. Father told me to take them to see my mother, who might like some bead work they had. The squaws also asked for some cloth and on the way I took them into Bill Roberts' at the corners.

The store was heated from a stove in the basement. A grating set like a register in the middle of the floor let out a great volume of hot air. A lady came in wearing a very large hoop skirt that touched the floor. She seemed to float along, there being no evidence of propelling power inside or under that skirt.

The young squaws were greatly interested as they had never seen the like before. The lady sailed serenely along until directly over the hot air register, when, like a balloon, she took flight toward the ceiling. There was such an exhibition of motive power that the lady forgot what she came to purchase. I was told she never entered Roberts' store again.

Then I took the brides to see mother and they told her of the strange sights they had seen. "She-mo-ka-man (squaw) no can walk in woods, no can go in canoe, wind no let her stay." They said a lot in Indian that I will not translate. To their wild-wood eyes that hoop skirt was as strange as a marble Venus. Truly hoop skirts were never designed for Indian wear and were no good in a sailing breeze.

Nowadays a good many go upon wedding journeys to the "old country" and spend a heap of money. With all their wealth they have not half the pleasure this simple Indian party had that summer with their sailing and camping; no trains to meet, no waiters to tip. If they wanted broiled whitefish or barbecued venison they knew where to find it without going to cold storage. Each day brought new scenes and adventures. When the ice of the winter stopped further travel by water they settled down with their tribes to the serious business of living.

Indian Baskets

One should have lived in Grand Rapids one hundred years ago to have a real understanding of the artistic handiwork of the Indians of this vicinity.

Basket weaving is an art in which the Indians of America always excelled, but each section of the country has differed in material and design. There is no disputing the claim that the Indians of the great southwest were the finest weavers in the world of articles for their special use, but the Indians of the great lakes country were also clever and artistic in making utensils.

The coming of the whites gave a new outlet for their work and they used it as a means of gaining a livelihood in the period of development from wild life to civilization. A student of Indian life in the fifties said that the Indians of that time were wrestling with problems of which they knew little or nothing and often were discouraged. "It was not enough to furnish Indians with subsistence and an agent to look after them. Unless they have more than that no tribe will ever make progress toward self-support. Something to do, and that something to be what he likes to do, because it brings him satisfaction and remuneration and nothing seems to furnish this so much as basketry."

Twenty-five years ago, Mr. Mason, the curator of the National museum, said: "After an almost fatal neglect patrons of Indian fine art are becoming to appreciate Indian basket work."

In my young days I watched the Indian chop the river bank elm and roll it into the water to soak; then after days, split it into sections about six feet long and with a wooden mallet pound the sections until the growth could be split into splints. Then on a shaving horse with wooden vice jaws they shaved it to even thickness and width and it was ready for the weaver. The squaws did most of the weaving and the form, pattern and idea was fixed in the imagination before the worker took the first step.

It is for this reason that basketry was most desirable for the development of the life of the Indian. The baskets could not be counterfeited, for there were no two alike; each represented the maker in her idealism and could no more be imitated than a white man could in fact become an Indian.

No one can weave the life of created things in nature in so strange and unusual manner as the Indian and no one can picture the wild longings of the Indian woman with the invisible as it is shown in her work; all her soul is embodied in her art.

I have watched the basket weaver, with hungry, half clad children about the wigwams, as with dreamy eyes and patient hands she wove in and out different colored feathers, sweet grasses and fern stems, staining them with the juices of wild berries. Each design possessed a meaning and gave the basket its own individuality. In all the colored designs that continue around the basket a space is left at the end as if by accident, yet it is done on purpose; this is the exit trail of life, to close it would mean misfortune to the maker. In the mind

THE YESTERDAYS

of the weaver every basket has life and is a part of the one who created it. They can tell their own baskets years afterwards and will caress them when they see them again.

And I have seen the squaws as they guided their canoes to the river landing, and with pack upon their backs went about from house to house in the city accepting cast-off clothing with which to cover their children or themselves, in payment for their patient labor.

Even as a boy I could not get out of my heart the feeling of resentment that the Sunday collection went to buy flannel shirts for the South Sea islanders when the soulful-eyed children in the wigwam on the islands of our own town were huddled in scant clothing about the fires to keep from freezing. The Indian boys and girls were just like white folks and had appetites and souls and bodies, and it seemed to me that something more than that thin soup called "sympathy," needed to be dished up at meal-time.

One day I saw a storekeeper give a squaw a small piece of salt pork in exchange for a pair of beautifully beaded moccasins that he put in a showcase with a price mark of ten dollars. His store was near the shipyard forge and I knew dad was handy and would back me up if I got in trouble. So I told the storekeeper he was a robber and would surely land in hell.

He may have believed me, for he agreed to give the squaw cloth for a skirt and I ran to mother, who never failed, and she selected the cloth and made the skirt for the Indian woman. We had many fine pieces of Indian bead work and basketry in our home in the early days and regret now that they have been worn out and scattered about as the years have passed.

One piece is still in good condition and that is a beaded medicine pouch of smoke-tanned buckskin.

The Indian Trails

It is well proven that the Indians of Michigan fought with the British against the Americans in the war of the Revolution. They assembled at Detroit, St. Joseph and Grand Rapids and without other food than that found in the forest and streams they joined the British forces in the east.

Those who returned brought knives, axes, some flintlock muskets, copper and iron kettles.

In western Michigan the three great tribes, the Ottawas, Chippewas and the Pottawatomies, made "Bock-we-ting," the Ottawa term for the rapids of the "Far-away water," their meeting place.

Wherever possible the Indian used the canoe for transportation. Often his birch canoe was the work of a year. Long journeys were made for the bark and the paint or dyes and the maker put his soul into the making of it.

All the country about the Rapids was blessed with brooks and creeks. When the ice in the river moved out in the spring these streams were alive with fish that came to spawn. An Indian with an ax could in a few minutes make a trap and scoop out a load. He kept only those he needed for the day and put the others back. This was the reason why the Indian followed the waters. It was a faithful supply train that carried his food for daily use.

Then there were the forest trails that by long use were well known to the Indian and followed by the whites in their first days or until land surveyors blazed section lines. The Indian followed the line of least resistance. He did not climb a hill when he could follow its base. He did not wade a swamp when he could follow the shore line. The sun his god, the moon his calendar, the tree his compass, he camped when tired and he sought and ate his food when hungry.

I distinctly recall some of the trails leading to the Council Tree on the west bank of the river. I followed some of these trails while on errands for my father or on my own boy's business and pleasure. The charm of the forest is still very dear to me.

There was a trail from the Council Tree leading southwest along what is now part of Butterworth-st. It wound about between the hills to Finnesy and O'Brien lakes and some ponds. Along this trail there were many springs where a boy could lie flat on his stomach and fill his radiator and

THE YESTERDAYS

the bank of the lake was a good place to rest in the shade and enjoy spring fever. Some of the best men that came out of the east settled along this trail and cleared farms. From the lake the path led to the Indian village on Sand Creek.

Then there was a trail that followed the river bank either way from the Council pine more miles than I know—upstream to what the Frenchmen termed the River Rouge, since corrupted to the Rogue river.

On the east side of the river the Ottawa trail became Grandville road and led to all southwest points. At Bass river it branched to the Pottawatomie country.

Going toward the east were many trails. Monroe-av. is the sophisticated offspring of a path to the Thornapple river, with a branch to Ada.

The trail that followed around the north end of Coldbrook hill was a puzzle to the white settler—a maze of hills, ravines and swamps, tangled in forests of maples and oaks.

In marking a trail the tree was not blazed; sometimes the wigwam was lost but the Indian never. If the day was cloudy the tree told where to find the sun. That was the god the Indian worshipped. In many myths he is represented as following the trail of the sun god. It is a fascinating trail for white men to follow.

Boy Scouts and Camp Fire Girls can follow many of the old trails and find happiness in the trees, wild flowers, winding paths and song birds.

On the banks of the river after a dinner cooked over a driftwood fire they can partly close their eyes and see in the smoke the wraiths of the rugged boys and girls of former days.

They may even, in a few places, curl up a leaf for a cup and drink from a spring that has never ceased to bubble since long before the silent Indian paused on his way down the forest trail.

Where Did the Indian Go?

There is in Indian life a charm that town boys of today like to follow and an invariable question that accompanies the recital of Indian stores is: "But where did the Indian go?"

There is in the question much that causes serious thought

and I do not like to put the white man in a poor light. Before the country was surveyed the white settler simply took possession of the land he desired and cleared it. Then followed the ceding to the government by the various Indian tribes the lands of the whole territory, the individual keeping his land by right of possession. As the land was gradually bought up from the government by the whites, the Indians were left homeless, became wanderers and under the white man's fire water, a bad lot. Then the government made the effort to assemble and place them on reservations.

When the Indians of this locality were gathered for the west, agents were paid so much a head and all the worthless whites, half-breeds, and squaw men, were inflicted upon the pure bloods, who really made good farmers and high-grade citizens. Many Indians of the Grand river valley were put on the reservation near Pentwater, which was much better than sending them west and many were able to take up lands under the homestead law.

Here is what I know about the going of one, and something of a few other individual Indians. There came to the Rapids every spring in the fifties a full-blood Pottawatomie boy about my age named Crow-Wing. He came from the Kalamazoo country by way of the Thornapple trail, which is still plain today, running through Charles Holt's place near Cascade. In the winter this boy's father set a line of traps on the river and borders of the small lakes to the south and sold his furs to Rix Robinson. In the summer he had a garden patch and a fish-jack and spear, spending his nights on the river and his days dreaming in the shade of the trees where the water rippled between the rocks.

Crow-Wing wore a red bandana handkerchief for a cap—so the white hunter would not shoot him for a deer by mistake—large brass earrings and carried about the odor of fish and muskrat blended with smoke. He was like any other boy, always hungry and mother's side door supply was unlimited.

In the second year of the Civil war he married an Ottawa Indian girl. With a rifle made by Solomon Pierce, the best gunsmith in the state, he spent several days shooting at a tar-

THE YESTERDAYS

get on the river bank, below the city and qualified as a sharpshooter in Berdan's famous regiment. There were more than two hundred Indians in the regiment. Men were proud to be called a Berdan and no better Americans than the Michigan and Wisconsin Indians wore the blue of the Union army. There is one place where many of the Indians have gone. They sleep in the southland.

Crow-Wing came home from the war and Uncle Sam gave him as part pay for his service a quarter section on the plains of Kansas, where there was not a tree in sight and the nearest stream of water a day's journey away. There in the shade of a mud-walled hut he died of homesickness.

If Uncle Sam could recall those days he would give Crow-Wing a deed to a bit of land on the Thornapple, with a few fish-hooks and some packages of congressional garden seed.

The white man would not then have reason to blush when the school boy asks him what became of the Indian. Most of his tribe have gradually faded away along with the forests, the deer, the pigeon, and other free things that were so native to his life. But it may be some consolation to know that of those who still exist some seem on the upgrade and coming back in high powered cars.

The Musk-e-Goes

It is well known, in the history of Michigan, Wisconsin and Minnesota that more than two hundred years ago a tribe of Indians occupied the Muskegon river country. They were known as the Musk-e-goes—"the people of the low country," or swamp people. Musk-e-go was also the name of the tamarack tree, native to the low lands.

In all there were nineteen tribes occupying the different valleys about the great lakes, each one bearing a name significant of its locality or its people.

Thus the Macatawas were the people of the black or dark water—hence Black lake and Black river.

The Pottawatomies were "those who kept the fire." They carried it about with them in compliance with a tradition that God had given them the fire and told them never to let it go out. Kalamazoo was their term for "boiling water," the rapid, bubbling river.

Man-is-tee is the Ottawa term for River of the White Trees, the sycamore, birch and poplar.

It is to be regretted that we have not preserved more of the Indian names. In naming new streets, locating tourist parks and camping places these terms would be most appropriate.

When the white man arrived they found the Indian had a name or term for all the rivers, hills and trees—in fact, a name for everything good in his life. He was grateful to the Great Spirit and found expression for his admiration of the things created for his welfare.

The Indian of the great lakes country used only four hundred words to express himself, the white man had thousands, and yet the white man found dozens of "Sand creeks" in Michigan and hundreds of "Mud lakes," where fish, water lilies, cattails, ducks and blackbirds lived. But the Indian, if he named any or all of these, saw not the mud or sand; he coined a term—or combination of words—that conveyed a sense of his pleasure or satisfaction. For instance, our various whitefish lakes and rivers were to the Ojibway, Ude-Kumaigs. One beautiful lake called Deer, to the Chippewa was Squaw-an-ga-nong, "the water of the two hills"; our own Grand river the O-wash-to-nong.

In that great waterway at Detroit is one of the grandest river islands in America. The Chippewas must have had some more appropriate term than the white man's curse of "Hog island." Not for a hundred years did it come back to life. Today it is the glory of the river and its French designation, Belle Isle, is a good term and I hope it will stick. It was a sharp jump from the river and its French designation, the Rouge (Red) that comes into the Grand at Plainfield, but the second jump made it the Rogue river of today. There was an unfortunate reason for this and it was clinched when one of its sawmill villages was named Gougeburg. It was one of the happiest little rivers in the state until the mill men came with their canthook names and rolled all the romance out of the stream.

I hope some of the nature lovers who are now building homes along its winding waters will dig up an old Indian name or two and so restore a little of its primitive "non-se"—"come from God." Michigan will never get full value from her lakes and rivers until its Indian commission renames or restores the names of many lakes and streams.

A Day on the Olive Branch

One spring morning in 1857, drifting away from the pier at the yellow warehouse, the steamer Olive Branch set forth for the Haven with a cargo of package freight, a top deck loaded with passengers, and Capt. Robert Collins, Pilot Tom Robbins and Cook Jim Dailey, with a full crew of husky Irishmen. We were soon winding between banks heavily wooded and bordered with wild fruit trees in full bloom—plum, cherry, crab and thornapple—all festooned with wild grape vines.

At the dock of Hovey's plaster mills a hundred barrels of land plaster were taken aboard. Then angling across the river we were against the bank at Grandville, the place nature intended should be a town site. The settlement got an early start with some of the best men who came out of the east in those pioneer days. Here we left package freight and took aboard a few passengers.

At Haire's landing we gathered up a lot of maple sugar in tubs and a pile of slabwood for the boilers.

At the mouth of Sand Creek, where there had once been an Indian village, we added a couple going to the Haven to be married. Coming down from the upper road they crossed the creek on a tree footbridge and the young lady had taken a tumble and had to swim out.

They built a fire to dry out as well as to signal the boat. Once aboard the women passengers fitted the young woman out in dry clothing and the couple were seated at the captain's table for the noon meal. The bride-to-be was game all right. She had come west to teach the Sand Creek school, but the first month she found a better job and the log shack's pupils had a vacation.

At the Blendon hills two families of Hollanders all wearing wooden shoes, were met by a man with a yoke of cattle. Their goods were piled high on his cart and the boat tooted a goodby as they trailed away into the forest.

It was a short run to Lamont, a beautiful place so spread along the bluffs—for every man wanted a home on the river front—that it looked four miles long and four rods wide.

All the morning a couple had occupied a bench on the top deck in front of the pilot house. The man smoked a fancy shaped pipe and they talked only in German. Lamont evidently touched his heart and with arm outstretched he recited "Bingen on the Rhine." I did not understand then as I did in the Civil war days, when I served with men who often in battle days sang of "Bingen on the Rhine."

There have been many changes since those days, but time cannot blot out pretty Lamont as it looked to me in my boyhood.

At Eastmanville Mr. Eastman came aboard with a party of ladies and gentlemen. The ladies were carrying many things made by the Indian women of the vicinity, beaded belts and beaded money bags; some had traveling bags of smoke-tanned buckskin ornamented with native dyes and woven designs of porcupine quills. The freight taken here consisted of many packs of ax helves shaved out of white hickory.

The long dining table was crowded at the evening meal. Capt. Collins toasted the bride-to-be who was garbed in the best that several "carpet sacks" afforded.

At the landing at Bass river Mr. Eastman took charge of the dining cabin and with song and story the Olive Branch rounded Battle point, paddling past great river bottom meadows of cattail and wild rice, from which flocks of wild duck came swirling overhead.

There were many inviting channels and waterways and the pilot needed to be well informed.

As we neared the Haven the sun in the golden west disclosed smoking mill stacks, forests of ship masts and drifting sand dunes. Beyond was a great sea of white caps. This was the end of a "perfect day."

The First River Steamboat

History informs us that the first steamboat to navigate Grand river was built here and launched at the foot of Lyon-st. It was christened the Mason and was presented by Gov. Stevens T. Mason with a stand of colors.

History and tradition both figure in the life of this boat. Tradition tells that a sprinkle of whisky instead of champagne wet its bow since the people of 1837 had not acquired a champagne ideal.

The craft was fitted with the engine from a boat that was wrecked coming around Lake Michigan. This engine was conveyed from the Haven in a pole boat. The Mason's first captain was William Kanouse, a Frenchman, and he had a French crew. The trial trip was made to Grandville and the second one up river to Lyons. Steam whistles had not been invented and Alanson Crampton stood upon the deck in front of the pilot house with a bugle, which was really more appropriate to the occasion. Can you not imagine how the people who had settled along the river and those who were coming down in canoes and on rafts were startled by the notes? It might have been the coming of the Angel Gabriel so far as they were informed.

There is no record that the Mason paid dividends in cash, but what it missed in that way it made up in development.

The first season was freighted with excitement. The spring of 1838 came in with a freshet. The Mason, which had wintered in the eddy of a driftwood jam near the shipyard at the foot of Lyon-st., was carried down stream by the ice and stranded near the present location of the Union station. The water, after playing this joke, subsided, leaving the steamboat among the cedars, willows and cattails. It was an invasion of bullfrog territory and before the boatmen could finance relief work the spring sun brought all the pests native to the swamp. Many of the men who did river work had a holy horror of snakes, also of fever and ague and even the inspiration of whisky and boneset tea failed to liberate the Mason.

Every day the boat settled deeper into the mud. One tradition that along in the fifties became history is that public leaders finally made a "bee". All the men, horses and oxen in the settlement were assembled and a corduroy road made through the swamp growth to the river. Demi John came also and a Frenchman lead the chanty that kept the workers in unison.

But the Mason again afloat cut all sorts of capers; was lost once in Beech tree channel, and went astray in Pottawatomie bayou, spent many nights on sand-bars and in 1840 was wrecked at the mouth of Muskegon harbor. With the wreck passed all but the memories of the river, the melodies of the chanty man, the echoes of the bugle from beyond the river bend, the glimpse of the Indian in his canoe seeking shelter from the swells in the mouth of a creek, the greeting of the settler who came to the landing for his mail. If he did not have a shilling to pay the postage the captain trusted to his honesty or accepted four-foot wood for his boilers in exchange. Steamboat life on the Grand was comparatively safe, even though erratic, but in the final wrecking on open water several lives were lost and as a moral we offer Mr. Drummond's advice:

"Now all good steamboat sailor men,
Take warning by that storm
And go and marry some nice French girl
And live on one big farm.
The wind can blow like hurricane.
And suppose she blow some more,
You cannot drown on Lake Michigan
So long you stay on shore."

The Old River Fleet

The first work my father did on coming to the Rapids in 1854 was the forging for five canal boats for the Illinois canal. They were launched in a basin at the foot of Lyon-st. and when completed towed to Chicago by way of the Haven. The boats then on Grand river were the Michigan, Empire, Algoma and

THE YESTERDAYS

Humming Bird, below the city and the Porter and Kansas above. The first dam had been built and the boats below the rapids came as far as the shipyard at the foot of Lyon-st. during the spring months when the water was high. The boats above docked at the head of the rapids about where the Grand Trunk bridge now spans the river and ran upstream as far as Ionia.

These boats were mostly side wheelers, flat bottomed and of light draft and they burned mill slabs or four-foot cord wood for fuel. They had accommodations for about fifty passengers and carried a cargo of package freight. The Humming Bird was a regular freight carrier built on two scows decked over with the paddle wheel between.

There is a tradition that the engineer of this boat made a practice of hanging his hat on the safety valve and one day in a burst of speed it blew up just before it reached the city. On board was a cargo of Illinois Red Eye and Cyclone Buster from Missouri. Some of this stuff blazed when it came in contact with the river water and the next run of mullet, the story ran, had red noses. The fishermen claimed it was due to the spread of the Humming Bird's cargo; others said it was a fish story circulated by John B. Goff, a temperance advocate who was stirring up the people about that time.

Later came the Pontiac, Nawbeck, the Forest Queen and that floating palace, the steamer Olive Branch—a regular Mississippi stern wheeler; staterooms with lace curtains, cabins and carpets on the top deck and a dining room that looked like a banquet hall. Jim Dailey, the chef, won the gold medal as best cook on the river. The dinners he set up were a drawing card that assured a capacity load nearly every summer day.

When the railroad was completed the great treat to wife and children was a trip via the Olive Branch to the Haven and back by train in the evening—an all-day excursion with good dinner, beautiful river scenery, the charm of the great lake and its wonderful sand dunes. If the weather was right some stayed over for a moonlight ride on the lake and an up-river return next day.

River steamers multiplied and prospered until Grand

Rapids looked like a seaport town. One morning Shantytown opened its eyes to find a full rigged sloop snubbed at its dock. It had come up on high water loaded with mill machinery. Shantytown bubbled over with amazement and prosperity. Even the cattails along the outlets lifted high their heads.

Until the Humming Bird blew up it wintered in the eddy near the shipyard. The rest of the river fleet lined up on the inside channel from the foot of Lyon-st. to Robards island with painters and ship carpenters busy with repairs for the next season.

A Honeymoon on a Raft

In 1858, Joe Simoneau, my good friend, came out of Flat river as captain of a lumber raft fleet. Joe was fond of pea soup; otherwise we thought well of him. While getting his fleet in sections over the rapids, which required several days, he met and surrendered to Juliette LaFlambeau, who was pastry cook at the Rathbun House, where her entire time was given to the making of dried apple pies and bread pudding.

Travel from down east was heavy and after the supper dishes were cleared away the Rathbun guests danced in the dining room. Juliette was a great dancer. Besides she told Joe she made good pea soup. What other good things she could make cut a small figure. She eloped with the captain and the guests of the hotel were left to the mercy of stewed pumpkin for dessert.

There being no school, with a boy chum I had been helping Joe and his crew of four French raftsmen pick up stray shingle packs that had washed off the rafts while coming through the rapids. Joe engaged us to make the journey to the Haven, where the fleet would be broken up and loaded on schooners for the lakes. We were to take our blankets, shotguns, fishing tackle and canoe and make ourselves useful along the way. With shingle packs we built a cabin for ourselves at the back end of the fleet. The raftsmen made one for themselves on the front and in the middle a fine one all roofed over with lumber for the captain and his bride.

We boys admired Joe for his good sense in getting such a prize, for in her pink dress Juliette was as pretty as an apple tree in bloom. But she went about mostly in a red flannel petticoat, for as she explained, she had taken no time to pack her clothes, "and Joe, he would get her trunk and back pay when he returned."

The raftsmen did all the dangerous work. We boys shot the game, caught fish and foraged for fruit, milk, butter and eggs, while the bride wrestled with the soup kettles and frying pans. A pack of shaved shingles served for plates and made good kindling. Knives, forks, spoons and drinking cups were the only things to wash.

The captain had besides an extra shirt, a fiddle, one of the boys a mouth organ and the other "bones." Juliette played a jew's-harp when she was not cooking, and sang a mixture of French and English—lacking the proper English she filled in with French.

Everything went well until a head wind tied us up at the mouth of Bass river. We were as happy as a flock of blackbirds in a newly-planted cornfield till we foragers went to a pasture and milked a farmer's cow. There was a bull in the pasture. We gave him a wide leeway for he appeared not to be very friendly and our judgment of him proved correct. Unobserved he followed us back toward the raft, where Juliette was dancing about in her red petticoat. All unannounced there came a bellowing from the river bank and as the bull charged, everybody in wild alarm made a dash for life. Juliette ran to the far side of the raft and took a header into the stream followed by the bull, but his red flag went out of sight in the water and he clambered over to the opposite bank. Juliette was fished out of the stream and Joe was so mad that he took our shotgun and crossing in a canoe fired three charges of bird shot into the brute's hide.

A few days later the fleet was snubbed at the Haven. The captain gave a banquet in the railway dining room that was banked up in a sand dune on the north side of the channel. A stiff gale blowing drifted every dish full of sand. The captain and crew returned to the Rapids by steamboat. We boys elected to paddle. We had ammunition and fishing tackle, but no money, and needed none.

Joe and Juliette made a farm up Flat river way and their cabin on the river bank became famous for its pea soup.

Early Council Days

Baxter in his history of Grand Rapids says: "The common council room was erratic in its wanderings." In 1853-55 it was the office of Recorder Bement, in the Taylor building at the foot of Monroe-st. The entrance to the council room was, by the way, a narrow outside stairway running from the sidewalk through the floor of a balcony. On one occasion this balcony became overloaded with people and gave way, carrying the stairs with it.

The council was to meet the following evening and the clerk, Peter R. L. Pierce, was on hand early, as was his habit. Taking in the situation he procured a light ladder and mounted through the window into the council room. When the aldermen arrived Pierce stood peering complacently through his gold bowed spectacles and blandly invited them up, having thoughtfully pulled the ladder in after him. There was a scene of much merriment. The city fathers, seeming to be impressed with the urgency of their duty as never before, were equal to the occasion. They procured another ladder and ascended council-ward, followed by many citizens, so there was an unusually full meeting that night. I am not certain whether Wilder D. Foster or Thomas B. Church was the mayor. I am inclined to think it was Mr. Foster, for Mr. Church was too heavy to climb ladders and enter through the narrow windows of those days.

Peter R. L. Pierce, the clerk, was the wit of the town and I imagine this session of the council was followed by a symposium. At these annex meetings men could talk in the dialect of the street and not be accused of lack of official dignity.

The aldermen of that time were Dr. Charles Shepard, Martin L. Sweet, Benjamin B. Church, E. H. Turner and Dr. Phil Bowman. Imagine if you can that body of men coming after midnight down a ladder from a window in so crooked a locality. As there were no street lights they probably were not identified by prowlers as they wended their way homeward.

THE YESTERDAYS

Judging from Baxter's history the common council must have moved its meeting place every time the rent became due. The salary of mayor and alderman was one dollar per annum. They were expected to do a lot of work and go to church every Sunday. How a man who had spent an evening in a close room above a saloon where men cast the dregs from beer mugs on a sawdust carpet and smoked Kill-i-kin-ick in clay pipes, could fumigate his Sunday suit was often a subject of debate. Mr. Pierce, so says tradition, suggested the best way was "move out before you move in." This inspired Ald. Bowman to burn a cotton rag at the desk of the clerk—at that date the latest fad in fumigation. The clerk replied that it might be effective in case of smallpox, but he had his doubts when applied to the Corners.

Judge Bement's office was greatly inconvenienced by the fall of the balcony, for it was this building that prevented Canal-st. going further south and from the balcony he witnessed the start of many a disturbance and was enabled to decide the case before the participants had arrived in court.

Tradition does not tell what caused so large a crowd at court as to overload the balcony and break down the outside stairway, but the greatest loss to the court was the judge's renowned meerschaum pipe. He offered a reward for its return, but it must have found its way to the river for the Indians reported later finding of many deceased suckers along the river bank.

Little Stories of Old Grab Corners

All the activities of the town, good, bad, and indifferent, centered about Grab Corners in the sixties. There were many fine stores and some very good buildings. There were also two justice courts, half a dozen dives, two chuck-a-luck games, some poker rooms, several basement bars where men drank whisky out of tin cups and where it was the rule to throw a drunk into the alley, leaving it to the police to come along and pound the soles of his boots as a test of life. If he kicked they carted him to the lockup, if he did not they sent for the coroner.

Shortly after our return from the war, Bob Wilson and I were standing guard at the corners, hating Crawford Bros. store with its red, white and blue checkerboard front. We called it Joe Wheeler's flag because it made us fighting mad. Down Monroe-st. came a farmer driving a yoke of cattle. Perhaps they didn't like the checkerboard either, for they became frightened and ran away, dumping the wagon and contents upon Mr. Shoemaker, superintendent of the Hydraulic Co., who was in a ditch mending a leaky water pipe. Warren Mills, the heaviest man in the town, was bossing the job and he called the farmer a "dash fool." The farmer yelled, "Well, maybe I am, but I don't like to be told about it," and he applied his ox gad to the fat man's legs in a way that was scandalous. Mr. Mills was not of a running build and hastily found refuge in the Rathbun House.

One other summer day a farmer came down Monroe-st. with a large load of hay. At the corners he unhitched in the middle of the road and drove the cattle down to the Pearl-st. river bank for a drink. The street was blocked from three ways. Teams could not pass so they headed into the hay and fed up while their drivers entered nearby places to discuss the State of Maine dry laws, which many feared might come this way.

That load of hay was "fed-up" about where the crossing officer now whistles his "step lively." If the owner's cuss words when he returned could be repeated they would keep traffic in line for a week.

Then came the time when the writer was the foreman of No. 3 fire company. An alarm one day brought us to the corners, where we found the fire was in the attic of the building that blocked the way from Canal to Monroe-st. The company being fire fighters, not wreckers, saved part of the building.

That same afternoon we were called back. This time the second floor was destroyed. A few hours later it blazed up again and it looked as if all we could save would be the cellar. About this stage of the game a prominent city official whispered in my ear that the building was past repair. We firemen took the hint and did not exhibit our former zeal and what did not burn was pulled down.

After this obstruction was out of the way street lines were untangled, river channels filled up and ancient landmarks disappeared, but the name the corner had acquired through long years did not so easily fade away.

Grab Corners

As far back as the traditions of the Indians of the great lakes country can be traced, the Bow-e-ting—the Rapids of the O-wash-ta-nong—was the land of Manito, the Great Spirit. Its charm also appealed to the white man.

So far as I know Aaron B. Turner, the "Horace Greeley of the West", was the earliest resident to trace and color on canvas the surroundings and the outline of the first white man's cabin. This painting became well known and met the approval of those pioneers who built and lived in the cabin which stood on the bank of the east channel of the river, about where the National City Bank building is located. It is now hanging in the Pantlind Hotel, the gift of Mr. Turner's granddaughter, to mark the progress from the time of the little frame cabin that witnessed the first marriage of white people in our valley. It was twenty years after this Burton-Guild wedding that I came to the Rapids.

By that time Monroe-st. was a fair country road, sloping enough to carry away the surface water. From Waterloo-st. it assumed the line of a crescent with the river bank for back water and Prospect hill for foreground. If the north point of the crescent had extended one hundred feet further travel would have turned into an alley and been swamped in the ponds of Kent. Monroe and Canal-sts. did not meet on friendly terms; in fact, they did not meet at all. Canal, not so well drained as Monroe, came head on to the two-story Taylor building that at long range seemed to block the way, but upon close inspection one found that Pearl-st. gave an opening to the east over Prospect hill, where the Michigan Trust building now stands. Beyond was a pond.

This hill was a ridge of clay and gravel about seventy feet

in height that extended north from Monroe nearly to Bronson-st. (now Crescent) and has all been cut away. One winter morning as late as the seventies I saw some young society ladies sliding down the last of this hill in a wash boiler. This was on the Dr. Shepard property, where the Young & Chaffee store now stands. They were not conscious of a spectator, but I happened to be in the bell tower of the fire department that stood nearby.

To the west, Pearl-st. ended at the east channel of the river opposite the north end of island No. 1. Along the river bank, stopping in the shipyard, ran an alley on the north and with the steamboat wharfs at the south. In this alley the storekeepers emptied their waste. Dodging off Pearl-st. in the bend was an alley that afterward became the Arcade.

Not until after the Civil war was the title "Grab" attached to the corners. The city had grown about this medley of roads and until the summer of 1865 nobody thought the intersecting streets could be improved. Lieut. Bob Wilson returning from three years' service found a congenial job as reporter on the Daily Eagle. He fixed the term "Grab Corners" and all the wit, ridicule and sarcasm of his red head was turned on this concentration point of village activity.

Raising the Grade of Canal Street

With the building of Pearl-st. bridge in the late fifties began the raising of the grade of Canal-st., which up to that time was often under water in the early spring when the winter snow melted and the ice broke up in the river; sometimes in the freshet from June rains or even when there came a January thaw. Several springs Canal-st. was left strewn with stranded logs.

The street as far north as Bridge was built up with a fair class of buildings, but not until 1873 was the grade, which put the street above high water mark, completed. In the spring of that year the old blocks and stores on Grab Corners which had obstructed the straightening of lower Monroe had been removed, the first to be razed being the Commercial block which had been the center of trade in that street for thirty years. Then in May followed the Checkered store, the Tanner-Taylor building which had stood broadside as a barrier to traffic.

Shortly after this a night fire burned several buildings on either street and left the Lovett block, corner of Pearl and Canal, standing alone. At this fire I had a peculiar experience. We worked for hours and several times I entered a bedroom on the fourth floor of a building on the Canal-st. side—which remained untouched by flames, though all about was ruined. It was daylight before the firemen left and in the final inspection I was impelled to this room again. Everything was drenched with water and plaster covered the bed and floor, but in the bed sat a wild-eyed child just wakened from sleep. She had been completely under the bed clothes on my previous trips. I lost no time in depositing her on the hotel desk across the street. Before the morning was over this building collapsed.

Sweet's hotel, a four-story brick structure erected in 1868, was the best building on the street and in 1874 was raised four feet. Hundreds of jack screws were put under it and at the signal of a whistle were given a turn. Business went on inside without the loss of a guest or dish and the work of lifting took but four days.

It was a busy time when a trainload of jack screws arrived from Chicago, where they had been raising buildings, and all the stores along Canal-st. were lifted from the mud to the new grade. There were still a couple of livery stables and some blacksmith shops on the west side of the street and several vacant lots deep enough to retain ponds of stagnant water. Mosquitoes and ague were in evidence and smudges, quinine and whisky much in demand. But one or two stiff fires about that time, while disastrous, cleared away much that was not desirable.

Ministers used this "great uplifting" as a theme for sermons, illustrating the power of men who by all working together accomplished such great tasks. On the other hand many of the stories discovered about that time and still in circulation are as extremely muddy as the clay and marl of the river banks from which they sprang.

Thus the years changed the topography of the city. Prospect hill, with other wooded knolls, was carted into the lower ground. The west part of Sweet's hotel was built over the east channel of the river and the islands became a part of the main land. The shipyard and its forge disappeared, along with the ponds which were the delight of small boys both summer and winter. Springs that came out of the hills were turned into the sewers and brooks of clear water no longer found their way to the river.

Canal Street Jottings

Before Canal-st. was brought up to its present grade it was bordered by a variety of structures ranging from a single story gin mill to a four-storied brick block.

The roadway, sidewalks and buildings were all in harmony and nothing seemed out of place to the citizen who daily passed that way.

About where the big Heyman store is now, there was a large two-story livery and feed barn owned by Isaiah Peake. The west end of the barn rested on the canal bank and all the rest was on posts over a deep gully that ran between the canal bank and the street for some distance either way.

Capt. Baker Borden built this barn, using walnut, hewed from the tree, for all framework and had it not been for fires, the building would have lasted a hundred years. Hay was unloaded from farmers' wagons standing on the walk and pitched through the second floor doors to the lofts above. While unloading was going on the passersby walked in the street.

The adjoining lots had no buildings for several years and a side rail along the plank walk kept people from falling into the ravine, which made a convenient place for the barn sweepings which, had it not been for the spring freshets, would in time have brought the place up to street level. It also seemed for some years that there was no other place handy for castaway hoop skirts.

There were also in this low ground, stray logs and stumps

which refused to burn when the ground was cleared. Conditions generally caused people to boycott the west side of the street.

Isaiah Peake, the proprietor of this stable, was assistant chief of the fire department. He was also constable and had many a rough-and-tumble fight with the fellows who insisted on sleeping on the hay in his loft.

In the spring of '71 a fire started in Wilkins Brothers mill and extended to C. C. Comstock's mill on the bank of the river, jumped the canal and before it was stopped destroyed more than a quarter-million dollars' worth of property.

This fire occurred in the daytime, all the people of the city witnessing the spectacle and watching the firemen make their desperate fight to prevent the fire crossing Canal-st. and sweeping the entire north part of the city. When firemen became exhausted volunteers took their places.

Assistant Chief Peake had more than a fireman's interest, for all the savings of his lifetime were going. With a single line of hose from the steamer Caswell he faced the fire at the Canal-st. front of his stable. As Company No. 3 was rushed from another position the men saw the assistant chief who had lost his footing, with the hose pipe hugged close in his arms, gamely holding to the wriggling line, which finally carried him off the high walk into the basement. Citizens pulled the line back to the canal bank with the assistant chief still hanging on. He was rinsed off and after several helpings to "refreshments" reported back on duty.

The great ramshackle barn burned for two days. The heavy walnut sills with loads of smoking hay and straw fell into the bog and smudged mosquitoes for a week.

To many people this fire was a loss hard to retrieve but not so with Isaiah Peake. He resigned from the fire department, but retained the office of constable and became reception committee at the popular farmers' hotel across the street, where the country men arrived every morning with loads of produce and were treated to a drink by way of a start and Isaiah collected fifty cents each at night for giving them safe conduct to the lockup.

The west side of Canal-st., filled in and rebuilt, was much better for the fire.

Echoes of Old Dinner Bells

You may wonder how I recall so well some of the things pertaining to the old hotels. When I came to Grand Rapids, an eight-year-old boy, with unlimited demands for food, I lived for three years nearly opposite the Rathbun House and still retain a memory of the appetizing odors that drifted from the kitchen. The Eagle hotel was also near, but the smells less alluring. We had pork, cabbage and corned beef at home.

Our playground was not beyond the sound of the dinner bell of the National. In fact, the meal-time of the neighborhood was regulated somewhat by the hotel bells and when George of the Rathbun sounded the alarm it broke up our ball game and called in the kites.

George was a colored man about thirty years old. He must have drifted in on the "underground," as there were few of his race here at the time. He rather outdid the bell ringer at the National and one time when a concert troupe was stranded in the town the musical director secured a long, round bar of steel from Foster's and at father's forge constructed a very clever and musical triangle. This he suspended under the wide veranda of the National hotel from a piano wire.

Thus the National was able to send forth a call more in keeping with its delicious chicken pie. Moreover the breakfast call did not awaken all the babies in the neighborhood. But Capt. Shoemaker of the Rathbun was a progressive spirit and startled all the street by supplying George with a gong half as large as a washtub. There was no veranda at the Rathbun House, but George was equal to the occasion: a few bangs at the gong, then "roas' beef for dinner"—bang! "Taters and gravy," bang—bang! Then a few juba steps to several slight taps before the dessert was announced. But the great event was chicken dinner. Then the small boys took to the gutter and George gave a near minstrel show.

The National acquired one summer a colored cook who came by the underground route from Tennessee with his weather eye out for Canada. It was rumored the United States marshal was watching to take him back to Dixie. The boys were much in sympathy with the runaway—they liked his biscuit—and while waiting for the government official they practiced throwing stones at a mark.

Steel's Landing (Lamont) on the river was a station on the underground. One day a man with a soft hat and long whiskers took passage at the Haven for the Rapids. At Steel's Landing several farmers came aboard and when near Blendon Hills the stranger fell overboard. Swimming seemed to be good and Bob Medler, the pilot, did not slow up. Walking was not obstructed on the underground that night and the National lost its cook.

Capt. Shoemaker and his wife of the Rathbun House were among the very popular hotel people of a day when it meant something to be landlord and landlady, when the guests of a hotel were treated like guests of a home. Of course they did not become millionaires, but in their day people did not live entirely for the accumulation of nervous breakdowns.

Canton Smith, landlord of the National, used to tell the story of a man who was worth $4,000. He was so blooming rich that he ordered chicken pie for dinner every day. Dinners cost fifty cents, no tips. Once a down east boob left a half-dollar at the side of his plate and the waitress slapped his face.

In 1866 T. Hawley Lyon, at the time landlord of the Rathbun, entertained the survivors of the 21st Infantry. It was our first reunion and it is doubtful if ever a banquet table in the city was so perfect in its flowers and food. That night many of us made our first acquaintance with celery. We really had to be introduced to the stranger, standing leaves and all in a tall vase. With comrades from all parts of western Michigan, music, dances and speeches, the affair did not close until sunup.

The 3rd Michigan Infantry boys were also served a wonderful banquet and how grateful the people were to Hawley Lyon and his charming lady, who were made honorary members of both organizations.

OF GRAND RAPIDS

The National Hotel, the Site of the Morton House

Both tradition and history tell of a hotel built on this site in the year 1835, the Hinsdill House, a two-story frame building with a ballroom on the second floor. Four years later this was bought by Canton Smith, who renamed it the National and conducted it until it burned in 1855.

It was replaced by a four-story frame building painted white, with green blinds, which in turn burned in 1872. It was the "uptown" hotel for many years. By this remark I do not mean to cast shadows upon the other hotels of that time, they had a rating as do the hotels of today, but nearly all of the overland travel until 1858 came in over the Kalamazoo plank road by stage. Turning the corner of Division and Monroe streets the National was the first hotel.

And just a word about those Concord stages which had a nation-wide fame. The few remaining ones are traveling about the country today as curiosities with the circuses and wild west shows. There were relay points along the route where change of horses was made. Four and often six horses were used and were selected for their traveling qualities. The crack of the whip, the blast of the long tin horn, the high-headed horses plastered with foam and mud were enough to stir the blood of any boy.

Although the ride was through forests and along the shore line of lakes, and dinner stations served roast wild duck and squirrel pot pie, the passengers after a fifty-mile ride in a jolting, swaying, cramped-up coop, were glad to clamber down from the top or out of the crowded seats and find rest in the hotel. It was such a home-like place and the hand that the landlord extended was so cordial that few of the travelers sought any other place.

The wide verandas with their chairs on summer days, the great fireplace with its blazing logs in winter were the best welcome the city could give. Men gathered about the fire and smoked their pipes and the ladies came and listened to stories or to discuss the events of the time. The firelighted circle was the picture of contentment.

One winter night when the wind whipped the snow and

sleet into every hangout place for boys, Ned Buntline, writer of story books for boys, was a guest at the hotel. The porter went out to the shops and streets and gathered in all the boys and standing in the firelight with the youngsters sitting all about the floor, Buntline told stories of the sea and of adventure in strange lands with strange people. I was one of the happy boys.

But the finest thing about the old hotel was its landlady of blessed memory, who in all the years that her husband, Canton Smith, was the manager, was his helpmate—a woman then in the best years of life with a mother's heart and good sense. "Blessed Mother Smith," she was called. Many a man and woman found with her a safe harbor until they were on their feet again. The fireplace in the lobby was matched by the warmth of the stove in the kitchen on which a kettle of soup ever simmered and from which many a bum was fed and sent away to the hay in the stables.

There were no city hospitals or refuge homes—only the county house to shelter unfortunate girls from the storm—and many a friendless woman was helped up the back stairs to the servants' quarters and a bed. The only register of these kind deeds is kept in the hearts and memories of those who knew "Blessed Mother Smith."

In the city of New Orleans about that time there was another Mother Smith and when she left for heaven the people erected in her memory a monument of great beauty, one of the glories of that city. Our Mother Smith lives on in the heart of many a white-haired man of this town who as a barefoot boy played about the verandas of the old National hotel.

The Burning of the National Hotel

The period between 1870 and 1880 was one of many disastrous fires. There were but three companies of firemen, very poorly equipped with fire fighting apparatus. The horses and their drivers were paid by contract, but most of the men were part pay volunteers, the best lot of men to be found in the city.

The west side company, No. 3, consisted of young business men endeavoring to maintain the standing of that company won by years of faithful service in the interests of the community. Its standing as a social organization was of high grade. Pride and rivalry between the three companies kept these men in service.

While the city was making rapid growth in all lines and fire risks becoming greater every day the firemen were held down to old methods. The papers of that period were printing columns about the brave deeds of firemen in risking life and health, but it seemed to the heroes engaged that the common council was sleeping over a volcano that would some day rival the kick of Mrs. O'Leary's Chicago cow.

The supply of water as well as hose was limited. Alarms were slow in coming in. There were no reserves and if two alarms came in about the same time, the second fire must burn itself out.

When the alarm came in from the National hotel on Sept. 20, 1872, No. 1 company set their engine at a cistern at the corner of Division and Monroe. No. 3 found water at the corner of Ottawa and Monroe, supplied from the Hydraulic pipes.

The writer was foreman of No. 3 company and when we arrived the hotel was a furnace. Chief William A. Hyde directed our line to a narrow alley between the hotel and a brick building on the west, the hope and plan being to confine the fire to the hotel building. We did not know that this narrow walk had no outlet until we had gained the dead end at the north, a two-story wooden annex. With a four-storied furnace on one side and a brick wall on the other side, the walls and roof of the hotel fell and No. 3 was trapped. They had a stream of water from a line of hose that could last but a few minutes. The pipeman, William R. Utley, turned the stream on his comrades, who were trying to break through the lath and plaster of the annex walls, though its roof was already ablaze.

There was no panic. George Whitworth, the only man who knew a prayer, used the time in wielding an ax. Where he found it he did not know and to this day that ax is a mystery. Every drop of the water coming out of the hose was turned on Whitworth while he was chopping the hole through which we crawled, one by one, and escaped to the vacant lot on the north. There we counted noses and grinned smoky grins; none of us had breath to do more.

By that time the crowds on Monroe-st. were in a panic. Volunteers had uncoupled the hose and put in a new section and a stream was turned on the fire where we were supposed to be. It had no effect on the mass of fiercely burning pine. The strain was relieved when the company reported at Putnam's drug store below the hotel, where their burns were coated with linseed oil.

There were nine west side business men in that party. They were not so much concerned with their roasting as the fact that a line of hose had been lost. It was a bit of disgrace similar to losing a flag in battle. Moreover they were used to leaving by the front door and the idea of a crawling retreat hurt their sensitive hides fully as much as the blisters they nursed the following month.

Among the men beside Utley and Whitworth, were Leonard Bradford, Thomas R. Belknap, William Walsh, Anthony Hydorn, Milo Markham and Charles Swain.

I recollect no passing that was so universally mourned as that of the old National hotel. Its comfort and hospitality, the cheer of its fine old fireplace, were known far and wide. It was never quite possible to replace the old home feeling in the modern structure and the growing town.

The Public Well

Some time after the building of the Hinsdill hotel on the corner of Monroe and Ionia streets in 1835, a public well was dug at the intersection of the streets near what is now the Morton House corner. The exact date is not a matter of record so far as I know.

Tradition has the well forty feet deep, stoned up with field hardheads. It always afforded an abundant supply of pure cold water. It was protected by a curb and wide standing platform; the water drawn up by a windlass in oaken buckets.

It is not claimed that the song, "The Old Oaken Bucket"

had its origin here but the well was so popular during the forties and into the fifties that the old residents may well turn to it as they sing the old song at their meetings each year.

Before digging this well, drinking water was obtained from a plentiful spring that flowed from the side of the present Fountain-st. hill and angled across lots into a sluice in Ionia-st., then open under the veranda of the hotel and into a sluice that crossed Monroe-st.

When one studies the formation of the hills, valleys and trails it is easy to believe that the early fathers selected this place as the hub of the wheel about which would center the commercial city, but they did not have the foresight to reserve a campus, or circle, which could easily have been done. About this location with the first hotel as a start, were built stables for the stage horses, wagon repair shops, horseshoeing and blacksmith shops and sheds for the Concord stages.

The natural grade of the streets gave good drainage and while the spring furnished an abundance of water it soon became an open sewer, so this "town well" became a necessity and it was one of the busiest uptown places until late in the fifties.

I have no idea who paid for this well and its upkeep, only for many years Mr. Wilder D. Foster furnished free of cost the tin cups that Mr. Weatherly chained to the curb many times each year. Even in those days some people realized that if men could get a drink of cool water there would not be so many of them running into "tippling" groceries and that a public well was a better temperance lecture than "Ten Nights in a Barroom."

Eventually the Hydraulic company began supplying water to the business part of the city from the Penny springs, located in the rear of where the Logan apartments now stand, on Logan-st., between Madison and South Prospect-avs.

The company also curbed the spring on Fountain hill and piped the water into buildings and into the cisterns that supplied the fire department before the days of hydrants. This spring was not far from the school on the hill. When Charles W. Garfield was a student there he had but to step out of

THE YESTERDAYS

the back door into a forest where the wild flowers, birds and squirrels lived. How often did he get permission to go to the spring for pails of drinking water, and he tells me how he mourned when this gift from God was covered over and forever hidden from sight.

I do not recall what happened to the town well. To the best of my recollection it was filled in when the Morton House was built, about 1873 or 1874. But I do know that where I paddled my dusty little feet in a running brook in the fifties, and stood and leisurely drank my fill from the oaken bucket in the sixties, I now stop, look, listen, and then run like a scared rabbit for fear of being hit by things I'd never dreamed of in those days—and I am just sixty years ahead of the traffic officer with his whistle, for I've stood in that very spot and whistled my dog from chasing rabbits and "chickens" in the grubs down Shantytown way.

The Fisk Lake Log Tavern

From the days of the very first settlers of Grand Rapids there was a forest trail from the east which, as years have passed, has developed into Robinson road. More people travel this road in one hour now than covered the trail in all the first year of its existence.

The Fisk family were among its very first followers and in 1837 John W. Fisk built a log tavern on the site now owned by Ben West.

The Fisk Lake House, as it was called, was made from the timber growing on the high bluffs which bordered the lake. Across the road, north from the tavern, was built a log stable to shelter the horses of the travelers.

How welcome the blaze of the great stone fireplace must have been to men and women after long miles of travel on a rough road, skirting swamps, fording streams or winding about the hills through an unbroken forest.

Can you not imagine this man Fisk as he came from the east and looked upon the gem of a lake that for all the years since has borne his name? Fisk kept this tavern for two years, then engaged in other building enterprises. The two years following James Fosget was the landlord. His ancestors were soldiers from France, under Lafayette, during the Revolutionary war. The girl who afterward became his bride was a niece of President Adams and came with her parents from the east; the last part of the journey down Grand river on a raft of logs and lumber. She was then thirteen years old. After her marriage to Mr. Fosget she became the landlady at the tavern and was as fine a type of American womanhood as the valley ever received, and at least one of her capable daughters is living near Grand Rapids at this time. The Fosgets afterward ran the Grandville hotel and their history will sometime make a story by itself.

The log tavern was in time replaced with a brick structure and for two years was operated by Jerome Trowbridge, afterward by Napoleon B. Carpenter. If ever a man was born to entertain people it was "Boney" and likewise there was no man, woman or child who knew her, that did not love and respect Auntie Carpenter.

Along in the seventies the Fisk Lake House was a great resort for saddle men and their ladies. Many of the cavalry and mounted soldiers of the Civil war had kept their horses. The ladies of that day rode side saddle and wore long, flowing skirts, tight-fitting waists, military collars and derby or stiff silk hats. They rivaled their escorts in horsemanship and the straight stretches of road witnessed many a merry race; ditches, stumps, loads of hay and stray cattle were no obstacle to cavalryman speed. Many a sentimental soul lost his heart along the winding Thornapple river road.

The popular stunt was to stop and leave orders for dinner, then gallop to Cascade, follow the river road to Ada and back to the tavern where Pat McCool looked after the horses and Boney Carpenter served chicken and the finest steaks that ever came from a charcoal broiler.

Frequently the evening ended with dancing in the upstairs ballroom, noted as having one of the finest floors in the city. Mr. Carpenter played the "bones" and set the pace. So here is just a word of appreciation for the good old landlords and their ladies—the Fisks, Fosgets and the Carpenters.

THE YESTERDAYS

Fisk Lake and Pat McCool

When Boney Carpenter took over the Fisk Lake House it was quite out in the country. He also took over with the tavern Pat McCool, who as a landscape artist, worked with a spade. When not terracing the bluffs he was looking after the stables or working out the road tax. You will recognize by his name that Pat had an inherited dislike for snakes.

In the swamps between Reeds and Fisk lakes there was always a good crop of marsh hay which was cut for stable bedding, cocked up in the field and left to dry until autumn days.

There was a log crib bridge over the channel between the two lakes and a strip of bog which seemingly had no bottom over which a floating bridge of logs had been built. This bridge often sunk out of sight over night. You can identify this spot now by the fine road bridge bordered on either side by all the old junk and scrap iron in East Grand Rapids.

One of Pat McCool's jobs was to keep this floating bridge passable. There was little travel between the lakes but it was a public highway and had to be kept open. When Pat hauled in new logs to replace sunken ones he covered them with marsh hay which made on sunny days a bed for a great variety of crawling things.

Pat always went out to work with his clay pipe between his teeth and a song buzzing through his nose. One morning he had gained the middle of the floating bridge before a rival buzz warned him that he was an unwelcome guest; a big rattler disputed the right of way. Pat made a jump that unhappily landed him in a wad of water snakes.

People at the hotel said he came up the hill on wings, his warning shouts breaking up a crowd of the best poker players of the day. This is a true snake story vouched for by the landlady of the hotel.

When the autumn days came men went into the marsh and hauled the hay out on sleds until the loft in the stable was filled. Out of one load crawled a big moccasin. Pat was too good a man to lose, so Mr. Carpenter himself had to pitch all the hay out into the yard, no small task, as he also had a dislike for reptiles, especially at close quarters.

During the years the Carpenter's kept the hotel William Hentig began cutting and storing ice at Reeds lake. He bought from the Belknap Wagon Co. the first real ice wagon made in the town. It was drawn by a fine draft horse fitted up with about a fifty-dollar harness.

Pat McCool, stuck on that nice white and green wagon, made application to drive, but Mr. Hentig, very positive in language—he was a past master at profanity—refused, and hired a Hollander, a nationality more to his liking.

Almost the first trip to the city the wagon with its heavy load of ice proved too much for the floating bridge and it began to sink. The Dutch driver saved himself by running to the hotel for help and Pat was the first man to the rescue, but the horse and wagon had disappeared. There was nothing in sight but a lot of bubbles floating on a muddy pool.

I cannot tell you what became of Pat. The last I heard of him he was sitting on Hentig's doorstep humming a very common melody of the day, "No Irish Need Apply." It was a dangerous thing to do.

The Site of Hotel Rowe

Next to Campau Square the Monroe and Michigan-av. crossing has witnessed more changes than any other district in the city.

On the river bank in the 50's was David Caswell's woodenware factory, Hathaway's edge tool works, several sawmills and sash, door and blind factories. A short distance south on the canal bank was Squire's grist mill—the stone castle—copied after a mill on the Rhine, stone walls, gray and drab. Only an outside overshot wheel was needed to complete the effect.

This was a factory center with water power. The canal and river were full of floating logs, slabs and edgings which made, except for the cost of hauling, free firewood for all.

About the corners sprang up a colony of blacksmith shops where everything from horseshoe nails to heavy mill forgings, and from wheelbarrows to farm wagons, sleds, cutters and carriages were turned out, mainly by hand labor.

THE YESTERDAYS

Germantown might have been a good name for the corners about this time. There were Rasch, Heintzleman, Friebig, Rathman, Osterle, Schaake, Emmer; with Edmonson, an Englishman; Pat Cain, speaking for himself, and Gelock, "just over," by way of variety. The king of them all was Charlie Hathaway, whose father was one of Washington's generals in the War of Independence.

In the winter evenings the blacksmith shops were open until 9 o'clock, their charcoal fires the only lights the times demanded. The boys and girls sliding down hill always found a cordial welcome in Charlie Heintzleman's shop and the little girls had a special seat and corner on the forge.

Canal-st., now Monroe-av., north of the bridge, was a piling ground for pail and barrel staves and the east canal bank a line of dry kilns. Boys earned their spending money piling staves after school hours. Battles were frequent and Mr. Heintzleman would leave his tire setting on open fire on Canal-st. and appear with sleeves rolled up, shirt open in front, and threaten to drive the whole gang back to Shantytown. Many a man had his troubles settled out of court through Charlie Heintzleman's good advice. He was a mighty worthwhile friend to young and old—a stalwart, two-hundred pound one.

In time the smith shops were crowded out. A single track street car put an end to tire setting and piling lumber in the street. The Rasch shop gave way to the Rasch hotel (later the Clarendon, and then the Charlevoix) which catered to the log runner and mill element. Spike-soled boots made pulp wood of the floors; sawdust and sand answered for rugs and carpets.

Then came the time and rule of the saloon in this locality.

The river man looking for adventure could count from the northwest corner eighteen saloons, most of them with back as well as front door entrances and an upstairs annex.

Fires destroyed the better part of the mills and factories and things looked rookery-like and dark, even to the tunnel of the old wood-covered bridge.

But through the years there has been a steady pulling upgrade and now the Hotel Rowe, honoring the memory of a grand old citizen, is a monument as well to the efforts of the pioneers of the district. As a kindly suggestion to its manager, whoever he may be, have the menu printed in English. Indian, French, Irish and German have had their day on the corner, though a horseshoe might be a fitting emblem by way of good luck.

Shooting Under a Light on the Thornapple

One autumn day in 1858 I walked with Robert Reed Robinson, ten years older than myself, to the Rix Robinson home near Ada, to shine the Thornapple for a deer. The country was being rapidly settled and while the deer were numerous they were wild. There were no game laws and deer were hunted with dogs at any season of the year.

There were some sportsmen who roamed the forest not so much for the game they could kill as for the freedom and joy of the great out-of-doors. Robert Reed Robinson was one of them and it was the promise of a night when one's blood would tingle at the wierd sounds and hair respond to every breath from the dark shadows, that called us to the Thornapple.

Many present-day hunters in violation of game laws "shine" with an electric plant on their heads. Had they lived in the fifties they would have made, as did the Indian, a box with one open side and a hole in the bottom through which a candle with a grapevine wick coated with deer tallow and beeswax, was shoved up from the under side as it burned away. This box was set on a staff in the bow of the canoe, just above the head of the man who was to do the shooting, the shaft turning easily to cast the light in any direction. The Indian hunter had many devices which were copied by the white man. In the autumn the outer bark of the wild grapevine tightly wound into balls, the open end lighted and placed in the bow of the canoe away from the air draft, burned for hours without blazing. When the staff light blew out in the wind the grapevine with a few breaths was in a blaze to relight it—then again placed out of the draft. There was also an incense wafted out of this smouldering bark that killed the scent of man, the danger signal to animals. All wild life is charmed by a light. Many times have deer faced the headlight of a locomotive, with its roar and rattle of cars, till tossed aside. So they stand in the water or on the river bank, unless they get the scent of man, their eyeballs of fire making them an easy mark for the hunter.

That night was my first under a light. Rix went with us. I was only a passenger. There was not a word spoken—no splash of paddle. Bits of fog lifted from the water and floated away, rabbits raced about on the banks, flocks of ducks went up with a whir almost from under the boat. At one place two men in a skiff with a jack light were spearing bass and pike. When we passed Charlie Holt's clearing his watchdog awakened the woods. Then we landed and waited for the moon to get out of the sky before approaching the big deer lick. It was near midnight when we saw two shining balls of fire and then the outlines of a doe not fifty feet away, then shortly two fawns standing knee-deep in a bunch of cattails. Rix never would shoot a doe and how glad I was. But soon two balls of fire so startled me that I did not see anything else and the crash of Rix's gun nearly sent the canoe over.

Making a landing a fire was built on the bank and a buck hung upon a pole, skinned and quartered and it was full daylight before we started down the river. While dressing this buck Rix told us an Indian never killed a doe unless compelled by hunger.

It was my first experience and the memory of it has never passed. Shooting under a light is an unfair sport but many a night in the wild woods of Lake Superior have I "shined" without a gun and had no end of pleasure. If the boys of today, who wish to become acquainted with the wild life of the woods, will use a flashlight in the bow of a canoe, with a companion in the rear who knows how to paddle, they will find adventure to furnish pleasant dreams for a lifetime.

In 1858 game was still abundant about the Grand river valley but people were wasteful of the forest life. Venison was served on hotel tables and dried venison was a specialty at Bentham's restaurant. The buck we killed that night was divided among our friends in the village and Rix added the pelt to those stretched on the side of his barn.

Turkey Shooting

In the fifties there were many sportsmen. Game was plenty and nearly every man had a rifle and shotgun.

The best rifles in Michigan were made by Solomon Pierce and his sons, George and Charles. Every part was made by hand from the rough material and my father made their forgings. I was delivery boy from the forge to the gunshop on the top floor of a building about where the Boston store now stands. Pierce's gun stocks were much more reliable than some of the stocks now sold; there was more oil in evidence on the finish.

Every fall brought great fun in the way of turkey shoots and raffles which took place at the homes of the farmers in the vicinity. They were usually an all Saturday affair that finished with a barn dance in the evening. To the farmer's wife belonged the poultry money.

The shooting was arranged in this manner: at the far end of the back lot a pit was dug and in this pit sat the farmer. On a bank above him was a box, out of which stuck the turkey's head. This was the mark. There were several ranges of different distances up to eighty rods with prices ranging from ten to twenty-five cents per shot. A man put down a dollar for the ten shots at thirty rods. Even the little fellow with a dollar had the privilege of ten charges with shotgun at the old lady's chickens.

When Jim and Tom Sargeant returned from a shooting match at Jenison they brought turkeys for their uncles and aunts and all the poor families in the neighborhood.

My father was some marksman and my older brother so accurate that he was limited to five shots for his dollar. If our five boys went, it took a one-horse wagon to carry away the spoils.

When it became too dark to shoot, cold roast turkey, bread and butter, pumpkin pie and cider were served and the fiddler played the hornpipe for the barn dance.

THE YESTERDAYS

Not all the men danced, for some of them belonged to the church and they spent the evening having a chicken raffle or disposing of their surplus shooting trophies. This brought about the only chance for ill feeling, some of them always complaining that they did not get a fair shake at the dice.

When the Civil war came along there was no trouble in filling the companies of Berdan's sharpshooter regiment. Many of them carried into service their turkey guns.

It is said some of those fellows as a joke, whenever possible shot an enemy in the leg. This required two others to carry him to the hospital. If the field was open the sharpshooter would get a crack at one of the helpers and that called for more helpers and there would be a straggling line of Johnnies going to the rear. But in shooting turkeys at any distance it was considered a disgrace to wing a bird; heads or nothing was the rule.

The business man of today chases with a club, a ball, which from dyspepsia and neglect, has shrunken to the size of a crab-apple. He is followed by a boy with more clubs. In the days of real shooting a man had nerves and eyes and one of Pierce's rifles. He needed no caddie; the bird found the ball.

I hope this may fall into the hands of Capt. Jesse Clark and inspire him to raise turkeys at the rifle range. With something worth while to shoot at every man in the battalion would get into the game.

There is nothing equal to the solid satisfaction of having a fat turkey hanging from the gun at "right shoulder shift."

The Head and Tail of the Sturgeon

As the whale is the monarch of the ocean, so the sturgeon was monarch of the river years ago. In the spring of the year it was in the nature of many kinds of fish to come to the "Bow-e-ting"—the rapids—to spawn. At this season it was not unusual to capture sturgeon weighing one hundred and fifty pounds and if Aaron Benneway was alive he could tell you of one that weighed two hundred and ten pounds.

All fishing with nets and spearing was done below the dam. The walks of Bridge-st. bridge were often lined with people looking at the fish and watching the canoe men spearing them in the water below. At night the scene was enlivened by the torches of the fishermen who with pitch-pine jacks, set on short staffs in the bow of their canoes, lighted up the shallow water for many feet about. With a man behind the light and another in the stern of the boat, both with heavy two-tined spears, they poled up near the dam and then floated back with the current.

There was one record night when Oscar Blumrich, still with us, and Aaron Benneway, long since fishing in the streams "beyond," went out under a jack light and brought in during the night seventy-two of the big fish.

The sturgeon had a standard commercial value: they sold for twenty-five cents, large or small. Some smart Frenchmen in Shantytown gathered the spawn, pickled it in salt brine and sold it as Russian caviar in eastern cities.

When properly prepared the fish made tempting food. Farmers bought them as a change from salt meats. Often a farmer would take several and pass them out to his neighbors. To dress them they were hung from the limb of a tree and skinned, the offal fed to the hogs and the spawn to the poultry. The meat wanted for immediate use was parboiled, to extract the oil, which was rather offensive, then fried with salt pork—a white, flaky fish, very good indeed. If not wanted at once the fish was hung in the smoke-house over a fire of chips that drew all the oil out and then put in salt for a day before the finish in the smoke-house.

Today we pay large prices for smoked salt water fish not nearly so good as the sturgeon. Many people utilized the oil of the fish for making soft soap, for in those days it was a poor cellar or woodshed that had no barrel of soft soap. Somebody always had an iron cauldron and over a fire on the river bank the parts undesirable for food were boiled and the oil skimmed off the water.

This oil also made very good lamp oil and was often burned in the torches used in night parades and even in the lanterns that lighted the streets. In some cases it made the "witch lights" that our mothers used; a simple contrivance of a saucer half full of oil and a rag wound around a hickory nut with a loose end sticking above the oil. Light this end with a wisp of paper started in the stove, for matches were not plentiful, and you had a light as long as the oil lasted. I remember my mother sewing on trouser buttons and patches by just such a light after she had her five small boys tucked in bed.

Sometimes men who had no tallow to grease their boots used sturgeon oil and it was the cause of many family jars when the old man came home with cold feet and stuck them in the missus' oven to warm. I knew one man who used it for hair oil, but he was intoxicated at the time.

In one thing the sturgeon was a source of joy to the boy. In its head was a semi-bone growth that had all the pliable, bouncing properties of rubber. The boy chopped this out with an ax, whittled it round with his knife and had a ball. He wound it up to the desired size with yarn from an old sock. This winding required skill that was gained only by practice. Then as to the finishing touch—if he could lay hands on an old bootleg of split calf or sheepskin in those days, for the outside cover, mother sewed it on—or if he could spare a quarter of a dollar he went to Moses DeLong, the shoemaker on Bridge-st., and came away with the finest kind of a ball, one that would bound clear over the house.

Men and boys played all the ball games from "two old cat" to hotly contested games that were the big event of the Fourth of July celebrations and a boy who could produce a fine ball was as happy as a bob-o-link swinging on a cattail in the swamp.

But to get down to the tale of our sturgeon. There came from down east a fisherman who had never speared a sturgeon. The Daily Eagle said he was the author of popular stories for boys and his book name was "Ned Buntline." He made friends with Bob Robinson, one of the best canoe men in town, and they started out to do the rapids. Buntline watched the Indians standing astride the top edges of their canoes and desiring all the thrills he tried the same.

They drew close up to the chute where the water came with a rush over the dam, tumbling about in swirls of foam. Ned

Buntline had been warned not to strike a fish any place except close to the head, but when he saw a huge sturgeon he got buck fever and struck near the tail. The electric shock that came along that spear pole and the rush of the waves sent him head first into the cold water. But he was a dead game sport; he clung to the pole and the fish towed him about the channel until Robinson got near enough to catch into his trousers with the gaff hook and pull him to safety.

A Fish Supper with the Sons of Temperance

The Sons of Temperance, an organization for the promotion of moderation in all things, especially whisky, occupied a hall on West Bridge-st. The entertainment committee planned a fish dinner and two of its members, who were experts, volunteered to catch a supply of black bass. The bass were biting up river at the big bend so there was no risk in making the offer. The volunteer fishermen were Patterson, a well known but little appreciated sportsman and Robinson, a tall, handsome, black bearded man, a graduate of the university, who always wore a stovepipe hat.

They borrowed the best canoe on the river and got an early start, casting anchor about four miles above the upper rapids. Landing two-pound bass was exciting sport and Farmer Jennings hoeing corn on the bottom lands, heard their shouts of joy and after a time invited them to join him in the shade of a river bank maple where they smoked a pipe in neighborly way. Said Mr. Jennings:

"The old lady is fond of bass. If you are willing I will take a couple to the house and bring back a jug of sweet cider I have in the barn. It is not good to drink water these hot summer days. I must tell you, I made a lot of cider last fall and forgot to put it in the cellar and it froze up. When I tapped the barrel all I got was a trickling stream like sap from a sugar tree in the spring. I left a cup on the sunny side of the barn to warm up a bit and along came a crow and dipped in his bill. Then he roosted against the door sill and sang like a bluejay. I filled all the jugs I could find and hid them away in the basement of the barn."

THE YESTERDAYS

So the fishermen joined the good old Irish farmer in what he declared to be the dew from which wild bees made their honey. Only the lure of the bass could call them away from that cider jug and when they finally hauled in the anchor the boat had a full cargo aboard. To be sure the silk hat had been knocked into the water a few times by the fish dangling from Patterson's hook, but they made the pond behind the dam in safety. Then Robinson spotted the chute where all the water of a busy river plunged in haste. That chute, the puzzle of raftsmen, had no terror for the man with the paddle and heedless of warnings from the bow of the boat, he made straight ahead.

In a twinkling the makings of the Sons of Temperance fish dinner, with rods, paddles, two fishermen and a silk hat were floating down stream in the mad swirls of the rapids.

Only the canoe and men were salvaged, but the women of those days were resourceful. They caught a salt codfish in the corner store and with peach blow potatoes and their fixin's the dinner was a success after all.

Winter Sports and Perils

Before the river bed on the rapids was cleared of its great hard-head boulders and narrowed by the west side canal—for this canal was a part of the river and its present retaining wall is entirely in the river bed—all the water of the river, except the small flow that passed down the east side canal, came over the dam and spread out in swirls and channels between the rocks in a combat for right of way to the foot of the rapids.

In the winter these great boulders made anchorage for ice formations and the entire river surface resembled islands of ice with narrow glades of clear water between.

In long spells of cold even the channels would close up and if snow covered the ice the canal gate would be closed and all the water coming over the dam flood the ice below and make it fine for the skaters.

Of all the winter sports skating was the most popular and there developed many expert men and women skaters. Most of the skates were home made. Factory made skates were just finding their way into the hardware stores and were distinctly American in style; short as the boot and blunt in taper, which was all right on clear, hard ice.

When the Hollanders began coming over they brought their skates, long in front and gradual taper. They were an innovation and looked odd, as did the people who wore them.

Our American girls wore long skirts and trim shoes while the Holland girls dressed in short corduroy skirts, heavy wool stockings and stout shoes that supported the ankle. When one of these girls went down, which was not often, she made a dent in the ice, but it was a modest tumble, while the home girl cut capers and blushed.

One winter day when the ice was all islands with narrow glades of water dividing them, that in the crisp sunlight looked like liquid race courses, the weather was at its best and all the skaters in town were out. It was like a carnival, except that it lacked the music.

The islands within safe reach were crowded, but there was one large glare place just beyond jumping distance that was tempting the daring. A party of Holland girls came down an open space like a whirlwind and going into the air one by one in their short skirts they cleared the glade and landed safely on this island of temptation.

This challenge was too much for the American boys and several crossed successfully and were soon linked arm in arm with the rosy cheeked, sensibly dressed Netherland girls. A dark haired American girl saw her beau cutting "pigeon wings" and doing the "long roll" with a pretty blonde and she tried the jump. When she left the ice her short skate caught in the long skirt and she plunged head first into the water with such force that she came up under the ice on the farther side.

In about a minute the crowd was frantic; all except a twelve-year-old boy—a "water rat"—they called him, who pushed his way through the crowd and followed the girl under the ice, where she could be plainly seen floating and being carried along by the current. Men yelled and women fainted or fell upon their knees sobbing.

Those who could see said the boy had caught her hand and

with his feet braced on the bottom was struggling for a place in the open.

It was a Holland girl lying on her face at the channel's edge who caught the boy's hand and pulled them out. Men brought planks and bridged the glade and the unconscious girl was wrapped in blankets and rushed to her home.

The boy refused to be helped out but waded to the shore side of the glade and climbing up to the roadway he hiked for the blacksmith shop. Here he was stripped and wrapped in a horse blanket while his clothes were drying. He was sitting on the forge by the fire surrounded by an admiring crowd when a big hearted Irish woman came in with a stew-pan of hot soup, saying, "There is nothing like hot soup to drive the cold out of his insides."

That boy had made his own skates. The blades were ground out of old mill files and he had worked many long evenings at the grindstone. The skates were fastened on his feet with buckskin laces. But Mr. Wilder D. Foster, who had a fine assortment of skates in his store, sent a pair of the best he had as a reward for his bravery.

In the late seventies there were several winters when the ice was unusually good above the dam, mainly because the drift ice was held back by the logging booms above the city. Hundreds of people gathered for the skating and in the evenings great driftwood fires were built along the shore. On holidays Squire's brass band played and added to the pleasure.

To skate on Reeds lake in those days simply never came to mind. It would have called for a walk of three miles before one could have put on skates and was just altogether "out in the country."

The Bridge Street Toll Bridge

The first bridge crossing Grand river at the Rapids was built from funds derived from the sale of a grant of six thousand acres of land given by the state. This open bridge lasted about six years. In 1852, a bridge company was organized to build a new lattice work, shingle roofed toll bridge. This is the bridge that came within my memory.

The lattice work was built of two by ten sixteen-foot clear stock white pine, pinned together by stringers of the same material at top and bottom. The uprights set at an angle, were pinned together where they crossed at top and bottom with white oak pins two inches in diameter. The roadway was sixteen feet wide and there was a sidewalk of four feet each side for foot travelers. The gable ends were boarded up and painted in large bold black letters, "Warning. Five Dollars Fine for Driving Faster Than a Walk."

A toll gate keeper's residence was at the west end, where he collected one cent from foot passengers, two cents from saddle men, three cents for one-horse and four cents for two-horse vehicles.

It was this toll gate penalty that divided the east and west side, much the same as Mason and Dixon line divided the north and south. This did not concern me personally, for I owned a canoe that would float an entire family including the dog, and I charged five cents for the round trip. At both head and foot of the Rapids in low water, teams could ford the stream.

Van, the milkman, drove through at the lower crossing until east side customers complained of finding minnows in the milk.

During hoop skirt days on those four-foot walks a lady's escort either dropped behind or dodged through the lattice into the roadway in order to allow another lady to pass.

Nothing annoyed Mr. Faxon, the toll gate keeper, more than the east side young people who promenaded the bridge on moonlight evenings. Within arm's length of the toll gate they would about face and two cents were lost.

For about four years the toll gate was the financial problem of the town. It might have continued many years more had not a fire started in Caswell's mill just at the east end and in a gale of wind the flames caught the bridge, Number Three fire company from the west side with their machine dashed through the blazing tunnel, but stragglers following close behind were obliged to jump into the river.

Peter Schickel and Lewis Martin were two of those who saved their lives by a leap into deep, cold water. The entire under roof of the bridge was a storage of cobwebs and dried sturgeon flies that flashed like gun powder.

For several months after that fire the east and west side were not on social terms. It happened during high water. Canoes and scows ruled and even faraway Mackinaw sent a fleet of fishing boats, manned by Indians, to help out until a foot bridge, that staggered along in the river bed, was built.

I earned so much with my canoe at the time that mother's yellow sugar bowl became quite heavy with copper cents and silver shillings.

The First Garbage Collector

Everything must have a beginning and to the best of my recollection this is how the collection of garbage began in Grand Rapids. In the early days nearly every family had its own cow, chickens and pigs and they very largely used up the household refuse. Not until the 70's did the city authorities make a determined effort to keep the hogs and cattle out of the streets and when they began zoning the town the disposal of garbage became a problem, greatly magnified because nearly every voter had livestock of some kind and the aldermen were taxed to the limit of their wit trying to please them all.

The first man to collect garbage had a pig yard on the commons at the north end of Front-st. He was equipped with a small two-wheeled cart with a barrel, drawn by a huge Belgian dog. The barrel made a seat for the driver except when it was full—then he walked.

Nearly every boy on the west side had a dog that watched for the "swill cart" and when half a dozen of them, large and small, engaged the Belgian there was a riot in the garbage department. This man carried a whip and applied it to the dog in a way that aroused the ire of the men of the Number Three fire company and one day they turned on the man a stream that nearly washed him into the next block.

For some time this man was followed by a trained pig which ran squealing behind the cart until the marshal ordered his pigship shut up.

For all this, business prospered until there were three dogs with carts and all the people in the vicinity of the piggery protesting. Then one day there appeared also from North Front-st. a venerable old man driving a lone steer hitched between the shafts of a two-wheeled cart and guided by rope lines attached to its horns. He came from some foreign land and unhindered built a shack of sidings and tin can shingles. He went about hatless and often coatless, accompanied by a daughter built on solid lines, whom the boys soon named "Sloppy Ann."

His piggery was a finishing touch to the atmospheric misery of the north end.

Richard Stack, the city marshal, lived at the corner of Leonard and Front-sts. He was supposed to be a peace officer but affairs moved very rapidly for a time, of which no official record was kept.

A string butcher bought the pigs of both parties and they seem to have vanished over the Alpine hills. Later on in garbage history when the piggery was located south of town the early residents, sniffing the evening odors, sensed the ghost of the Belgian dog, Sloppy Ann, and the steer, circling in from the dusk, and every owner of a good watchdog had him out on guard.

Kent County's Pioneer Jail

The county jail from 1852 to 1872 was on Court-st., on the west side of the river. I do not remember which was located first, the jail or the street. The jailer's wife's sister, the finest looking girl in the city, was the only one courted there.

The jail was a large, imposing barn-like building painted Venetian red; the front part a residence for James VanAuken the turnkey, and the cell block a two-story affair in the rear. There were no reception rooms and since there was no sewerage there were no toilets or baths.

The turnkey often on summer nights led groups with ball and chain attachments to the river where their outer black marks were washed away in the swirls of fresh water. Each cell had a straw tick on a bench, a blanket, and a bucket.

In the morning the prisoners came out in the yard with

their buckets and a scrub broom, to pump water from a well and make their toilets, each man anchored with ball and chain. During the day they cut with buck-saws the supply of four-foot maple wood into stove length for heating and cooking.

Mr. VanAuken was a tall man with a full black beard, an eye like an eagle and a pair of jaws like a bear trap. If he had worn rings in his ears he would have been my ideal of a Capt. Kidd. I like to recall him a few years later, leading a cavalry charge through a Tennessee cornfield instead of standing guard over this bunch of blear-eyed stragglers.

Of course once in a while the sheriff brought in a cattle thief from up Gougeburg way and that added a bit of excitement, but no matter how high a man's standing he had to clean his own bucket and buck wood until the learned counsel, who would look after his interests in the next chapter of his life, had time to go to court.

One summer day there was a horse thief among the group. His offence was well toward the top of the list and watching his chance he placed the chain of his hobble on a block of wood and with one blow of the ax was free to run. Jumping the garden fence he was on the road to Canada with Turnkey VanAuken in hot pursuit.

At that time all the west side of the city south of Bridge-st. was the Fifth ward. Chester A. Morey was the alderman with a salary of one dollar per year. Between pay days he shingled barns to meet expenses. From his high place on a roof he witnessed the race and scrambling down rushed into the road, swinging his arms as though stopping a runaway horse. They met head on; that's all the alderman remembered. Even when he came to he had spun around so many times he was dizzy. The horse thief made an uninterrupted escape to Canada while the turnkey helped Mr. Morey over to the jail to get the stars out of his head and repair the disastrous results of fulfilling his aldermanic duties.

The First Sprinkling Wagon

Thomas Sargeant, one of the early residents, was the owner and manipulator of the first sprinkling wagon and the merchants on Monroe and Canal-sts. paid for his service. Judging mainly by the memories of my early swimming experiences it must have been about 1855 that Mr. Sargeant lived on Waterloo-st.—now Market-av.—at the corner of Fulton-st. Nearby was a large sandy bottomed pond of water, where boys had a lot of fun with their toy sailboats and where many learned to swim without the help of bathing suits.

This pond headed in a brook near Baldwin's brickyard, located at the present corner of Fulton-st. and Lake-dr. This brook ran a wild race between the hills across the Ransom woods, now Dudley E. Waters' property, and down State-st. on its way to the river.

Before it was lost in the big stream it rested awhile to play with the boys. When all the other early day swimming holes are forgotten there will still linger in the memory of many granddads the happy hours spent in Sargeant's pond.

Mr. Sargeant had grownup twin boys. They were so near alike that he could hardly tell them apart. He also had a pair of horses that were the pride of the town.

When the dry summer days came, dust on Monroe and Canal-sts. drifted into the stores to the great damage of the stocks of goods. So about 1857 the merchants induced Mr. Sargeant to sprinkle the streets. He built a watertight square box, with a trap door on the top and a sprinkler spout at the lower back end, and with a valve operated by means of a piece of rope.

I have watched him many times as he backed down into the river at the foot of Fulton-st. and filled the tank with buckets, taking much more time and hard work than to sprinkle it out on the street. Later Butterworth & Lowe put in a force pump which filled the tank and was a great help for Canal-st. sprinkling.

For many years the street sprinkling remained in the Sargeant family, their tanks growing from this primitive one to the best modern equipment and their horses the finest in the city.

In the fifties sprinkling Canal-st. was a tough proposition. When the logs and stumps were put out of the way there was nothing this side of China to which a man could anchor in rainy weather and after a few days in the sun the mud turned to drifting dust. Lumber being plenty the roadway was planked with two lengths of eight-foot clear stock pine, which in a short time was standing on edge or end. The Sargeants through their years of service must have sprinkled on that street everything in the way of pavement from lumber to cobblestone, cedar block, pine block, cement and asphalt.

The city did not take over the sprinkling job until it had a water system of its own and even then some of the Sargeant family were employed. The first water pressure we had was put in by C. C. Comstock. He had a line of wooden pipes running from a reservoir on the hill to his pail factory on Canal-st.

The Police Patrol

In the smoke of boyhood memories I see the village marshal doing the scavenger work of our frontier town almost unaided. The city jail was on the west side of the river and Bridge-st. had the only bridge crossing the river. To the marshal it was a village of magnificent distances, for his chief source of supply was from Waterloo, Monroe and Canal-sts.

The men who built the plank walks on these main streets graded them on the high, low, jack plan. Going north on Canal-st. one went up three steps in grade in order to enter the "tippling" grocery of John Davis, then down two steps to reach the level of Dikeman's watch shop. So it was all the way to jail. When the marshal encountered game in Shantytown that was not shot in the legs he locked arms with the victim and hopped, skipped and jumped to the calaboose. If the victim's legs proved unreliable he was loaded into a wheelbarrow of the garden variety and at the ups and downs of the walk lifted by the heels.

Later an Irish buggy—or railroad wheelbarrow—came into use and still later the city council bought a two-wheeled handcart that could be pushed in the road. As business increased the marshal was permitted to hire any convenient dray at not more than twenty-five cents a trip. The two-wheeled French dray with the hind end dipped low was the popular kind. It was no great sin to get drunk then, but an 'elluffa joke to go to jail on a French dray.

As civilization and the lumbering days advanced constables were appointed to help the marshal. These guardians of the peace, armed with a club, pounded the soles of an inebriate's boots as a test of life and to determine whether a stomach pump or the coroner should be employed.

But in the words of Uncle Jasper "the world do move" and we jumped from a "twenty-five-cents-a-trip" dray to a thousand-dollar patrol wagon with matchless team of thoroughbreds. I can see the street in a fever of excitement as the brass trimmed chariot dashed through, its gong clanging, its bright buttoned driver leaning far out and urging on the best pair of horses that money could buy. For the moment business on the street was suspended, dentists dropped tools into their patients' mouths and ran to the windows, clerks in the stores found their way to the sidewalks to see "Black Maria" with its load of hard cider or "Milwaukee champagne" deadheaded to the station. Having arrived the passenger was dumped out on the floor and those horses which had saved the town were rubbed until they shone like silk.

Next morning the cause of all this celebration looked and felt like a battlefield. The judge said "six cents and costs." The clerks figured no overhead. I see in the smoke of memory one fellow who made this triumphant journey so many times that if overhead was counted he would owe the taxpayers enough to build a schoolhouse.

After some years police headquarters was established on the second floor of a building on the corner of Monroe and Ionia where the Grand Rapids Savings bank now stands. For ten years it was the unwelcome neighbor of the uptown hotel. Grab Corners, as a matter of economy and by all the laws of gravity of a wide open town, would have been a better location. Headquarters was accessible only by way of a narrow stairway that unfortunates as well as the officials termed the "misery trail."

James Moran was chief of police with a force of eight men,

the bravest lot of scouts to be found in the city. One of them arrested a drunk at the Detroit & Grand Haven depot, then in the north end—"Coldbrook," for short. He fought the officer every step of the way to the station and up misery trail. Said the judge: "Officer Conlon, what is this man charged with?"

"Drunk, your honor."

"But," said the judge, "he is not drunk."

"Well, your honor, he was drunk when I arrested him two hours ago."

Chief Moran was formerly a river pilot. During the Civil war he served as pilot on a Mississippi gunboat. He wore a full black beard, was a man of dignified ways and great determination and if he had been properly supported by the city council would have had a ground floor lockup somewhere off the main street and better sanitary conditions for the prisoners.

Street Lights

Grand Rapids' people did not vote on daylight saving back in the fifties. They used all the daylight there was and longed for more. In those days, girls were never seen on the street at night without an escort and boys were supposed to be in bed at nine o'clock. It was always nine until ten, but after that hour any boy caught on the street needed a good excuse for being there.

When it became dark, merchants hung lanterns outside their stores and people who traveled about carried lanterns with them. Prayer meeting night at the old church, on the bank of the river, found almost as many varieties of lanterns outside as there were kinds of people inside.

It was quite the proper thing for a beau seeing his girl home to use his unemployed arm in carrying a lantern. Lamps filled with sperm oil or any kind of fish oil and tallow candles were used in the homes. I am not sure what the "burning fluid" was made from that came to take the place of the candles and fish oils. Some people said it was imported from Hades. The lamps often exploded, giving employment to doctors and the fire department.

You will find specimens of the lanterns used at that time

in the museum or in the attics of old homes. Not long ago the writer was in the sitting room of one of the popular suburban hotels and over the fireplace there was hanging a nest of ancient candle molds. A young city woman present said she thought it was a relic unearthed from a nearby Indian mound. I did not explain that it might have been a part of her grandmother's kitchen outfit, for in pioneer days all the candles were made at home and the lighting problem was a serious one with the mother.

In Wilder D. Foster's tin-shop candle molds were turned out as rapidly as Ford's Eliza Janes now are. There was no change in style; it was quantity production that counted. But in lanterns there was a chance for the smith to show his skill.

There was one design that, with a candle inside, threw out rays of light to rival an eighteen-carat diamond. It was made of tin with conical top and punched full of holes like a nutmeg grater; the idea was to let out the light without casting shadows. Then an artist invented a square tin frame and put glass windows in it and that was followed by all glass globes.

Mr. Foster also sold candle snuffers for clipping off the ends of burned wicks. They were made somewhat like a pair of shears, except on one blade there was a box into which the clippings fell. Once I was spending an evening with Billie Westerhouse, a German boy friend, when his mother could not find the snuffers. The light was so poor that his father gave up trying to read his paper and called, "Well, Billie, come and pull off mine boots and I will go to bed. I have some leetle grabble stones in that boot all day." Billie straddled the boot and with the help of the other boot against his hips he pulled off the clumsy footwear—and out fell the snuffers.

Later came the days when candles were made in factories and sold in the stores and every home had a lighted one in the window at night.

It was in the fifties that the city first afforded street lights. Cedar posts were set up at street corners with a sperm oil lamp at the top. They were lighted at dark by the official lamplighter who went about with a short ladder. At 11 o'clock he made another round to blow them out. The council had to increase his pay he wore out so many trouser seats scratching matches on windy nights. There was a contention about the need of illumination on moonlight nights.

It was not until 1857 that a gas plant was completed and several stores on Monroe-st. were lighted. Although it was a November night when this was first tried out many people who had never before beheld a gas light went down town and gazed with wonder at the new luxury. Some old timers doubted the wisdom of the change. It was like shining in opposition to Providence and the moon. The city council studied the almanac and in contract for street light cut out moonlight nights and lights after 11 o'clock. The city did not save much, for the old lamplighter had the habit of blowing out the blaze while the gas meter remained on the job.

Between the fellow who blew out the gas and the coal oil, camphene and burning fluid explosions it seemed for a time that the good old sun and moon and Deacon Pengelly's sermons were the only reliable lights along the pioneer's path.

Near the end of the nineteenth century electric lighting became universal—so when you contrast our streets at night with those of your granddads some of you at least will feel glad that you did not live in the good old days.

Historic Railway Station

There is one historic building still standing in Grand Rapids which will not be forgotten by old residents but is liable to be overlooked by present-day people and that is the old Detroit, Grand Haven & Milwaukee railroad station in the north end.

In the year 1858 the first railroad train came rumbling through the hills from the east, the heavy down grade making it possible to reserve steam enough to blow the whistle in long, triumphant shrieks.

I remember this event so well, for half the pupils of the schools were there to welcome it and the teachers were busy the next day with the ruler on those who brought no written excuse for absence.

I do not know which came first, the train or the station

house, but the depot is still on the job despite the ravages of time and fires. It is about twenty-four by fifty feet and having had several coats of paint during the last sixty-five years is still in a good state of preservation.

In building this road the line of least resistance was followed by the engineers and that is why the depot was located at the extreme north of town. After many years the Grand Trunk railroad built a spur track and its present fine station down town. Probably as a matter of sentiment the old structure has been allowed to stand. It was so dear to the hearts of the traveling public. It seemed all the outgoing passenger trains departed before daylight and those arriving came after sundown and before the days of the street car (1865) the travelers rattled over the combination of river-bed stone, gravel and then cobblestone in a yellow omnibus or tramped upper Canal-st., which for many years was the white man's warpath.

Night trains ran on a regular behind time schedule and the men hovered over the old heater stove and used the floor for a cuspidor while the women curled up disconsolately on the wooden benches.

In the northwest corner of the waiting room was a lunch counter, where "slush and sinkers" were served. When those good old-time Scotch-Canadian conductors went through the train announcing, "Grand Rapids, twenty minutes for supper," everyone on the train who was not so fortunate as to have a lunch with him made a rush for the counter. The waitress was there providing she had not been driven off by an invading army of cockroaches. If she had survived, the compliments on the food she served usually finished her.

The only persons who really enjoyed the Coldbrook depot were the Burr Watrous log runners who gathered there from Flat river points, armed with peavies. They speared the sinkers from the counter with their picks and their boot spikes made the floor a frazzle of pine slivers. The benches and door frames were a mass of hand carving. Soft pine is so attractive to the average jack-knife.

This lonely place was almost as interesting as a circus when the trainloads of emigrants came in and shouldered their calamities for a two-mile walk to Waterloo-st., where they found wagons in which to continue their journey to the Holland colony.

Through this avenue came many of our statesmen to attend the political meetings of the day. They were met and escorted down town by hundreds of mounted men, lines of carriages and bands of music; sometimes by torchlight processions. James G. Blaine received as great an ovation as any one I now recall.

When the last soldiers came home in 1865 they were met at the old depot by all the town. There was no order to the reception. The mothers, sisters and sweethearts clung to boy and uniform and laughed and cried by turn all the length of the two-mile trail. Above all the hubbub and joy of that march I can still hear the voice of my little brother demanding that I go and give old John Winters, an English shoemaker, a licking for being disloyal. But I had had all the fighting I wanted.

Fifty years ago a ten-thousand-dollar depot, with a canary bird or two by way of variety of animal life at the lunch counter, would have put the north end on the map, but the order has been reversed. The homes, factories and business traveled out to and far beyond the shoddy little structure dignified for so many years by the name, Detroit, Grand Haven and Milwaukee depot.

West Bridge Street, 1858 to 1891

West Bridge-st. from the earliest days was an important highway. In the spring of 1858 unusually high water in the river, backing up through the lowlands, flooded the street from Turner to Stocking. I poled my large canoe for the accommodation of the public nearly five blocks, fare two cents. There being no competition as much as one dollar was earned some days. At that time there were few buildings on the street.

Down Stocking-st. came James Rogers, driving his father's oxen hitched to a farm wagon. He objected to the fare and started to drive through. Uncle George Barker, who had a farm on Bridge-st. near the hill and always came to town with a pocketful of apples, because he would rather give them than have the boys coon them, and Uncle Billie Stocking, who owned the farm at the end of Stocking-st. and whom everybody loved, were waiting to ferry over. They advised Jim to chain the cattle to a tree and get into the canoe.

But Jim used the gad on the oxen and about half way over the water was in the wagon bed, the cattle almost swimming and Jim sitting on one edge of the wagon box with feet raised to the other side. Then one front wheel dropped into a hole and Jim went backward into the flood. He did not come to the surface. The frightened cattle headed for dry land, the canoe turned back and Uncle Billie Stocking pulled Jim aboard. He had bumped his head on a wagon wheel as he fell overboard.

A few days later Mr. Barker came to dad's shop with a copper cent, which Jim had given him to pay his canoe fare, saying as he had ridden only half way I was not entitled to full fare. Dad said he paid too blank much, but Mr. Barker drilled a hole in the coin and with a long spike nailed it on the bow of the canoe as a mascot.

Thirty-three years after the flood Bridge-st. was above high water and paved with Hallwood block. The city will never see the like again, a pine block on a sand foundation. It did not last long enough to collect the tax for its cost, but what a glorious time the west side folks did have when this pavement for seven blocks was opened to the public on Aug. 29, 1891.

At. White may not be guilty, but I'll give him credit for this report of the opening, in a morning paper:

"West Bridge-st. was a magnificent spectacle last night seen from the hill on East Bridge-st.

"It looked like a mass of solid light. Jubilant in the possession of a pavement at least second to none in this city or any other, the property owners along that thoroughfare had spared neither trouble nor money to make their celebration a glorious one, worthy of their street and its cost.

"Thousands of Chinese lanterns crossed and recrossed the street in two zigzag lines while thousands more adorned the fronts of the business blocks and were strung along the outside of the sidewalks. The effect was dazzlingly, superb!

THE YESTERDAYS

From the roofs of the buildings which line the street Roman candles were shooting forth their balls of many colored fire and rockets soared among the stars in every direction. Crimson lights shed their bright refulgence upon the scene and added to the general splendor. In its entirety the scene was one which will long be remembered by those who gazed upon its glories."

There was a lot more but the procession must not be delayed.

A line of bicyclists.

Detail of Police. Lieut. Hurley.

Malta Castle band.

Carriages, city officials.

Polish band.

Company I state troops, Capt. Ed Bennet; Company B state troops, Capt. John Kromer; Company K state troops, Capt. Lampert.

Marshal of the day

The Hon. Ald. Doyle.

Mr. Doyle was mounted on a spirited horse. Over his shoulder, crossing his breast and about his waist a brilliant red silk sash. A high silk hat and white gauntlet gloves also featured. A sea of young humanity fell in behind the marshal, separating him for a time from the line.

There were three speakers' stands and upon one of them were Mmes. Lydia Harrington, Elmira Wheeler Dishman, Emily Burton Ketcham, Elizabeth Roberts Watson and Sarah Ann Davis, pioneer white pupils, who attended the first school in the locality.

They related things of school days and I had the pleasure of telling of canoe days and thinking it all over quite agree with father when he said the copper cent was too blank much.

Pearl Street Bridge

From Baxter's history of Grand Rapids a brief outline of the building of this bridge is taken: "A wood truss with lattice work between the roadway and the footwalks on either side with shingled roof—completed in the fall of 1858. This spanned the main channel of the river. The island and east channel were filled in to make a high embankment which brought the bridge and roadway to the grade of Monroe and Pearl-sts. It was a toll bridge until 1873, when the city bought it, and was for those days a fine structure which aided in the development of the west side."

Recollections of the toll gate at the west end may rob some persons of pleasant memories of the bridge, but not those who as young folks made it a happy trail on moonlight evenings.

The writer did not spend much time with the girls, but some other fellows a few years older did. The walks were narrow and when couples met the young men had to drop back or climb through the lattice to the driveway.

There should have been an ordinance giving "Shantytown" the south and Kent the north walk. If one had been in force Pat Shields would not have found reason to throw LeGrand Pierce of Kent over the railing into the river channel. LeGrand's girl was game and she met him as he waded out on the island below.

In the clearing up of the Mission land on the west side William Hovey reserved a grove of oaks not far from the old bridge and with benches, swings and tables made good picnic grounds. Hovey's grove was a fine place, but to get there every one had to pay toll. It cost an east side fellow four cents for a round trip with his girl. The gatekeeper was usually an old man, with wornout legs and foot races were common affairs. The girls in their balloon skirts were at a disadvantage on windy days and they could not jump through the lattice into the driveway, but the stockholders were hunting dividends and the life of the gateman was as bumpy as a corduroy road.

When the boys returned from the south in 1865 the town wanted to show its gratitude so a Fourth of July dinner was planned. The only place in town to set a table of sufficient length was on Pearl-st. bridge. The cobwebs and dust of six years were swept into the river and two long rows of tables

THE YESTERDAYS

placed from end to end of the driveway. They were loaded with all the good things the country and city afforded, roast pig, turkey, duck, chicken, cake, pie, jellies and preserves and, would you believe it, beans, beans, beans, rations enough to feed an army corps.

But how to get this to Sherman's "Bummers," Sheridan's "Jayhawkers" and Grant's "Mudsills" and keep it away from the home guard, had not been planned. Before noon the streets at both ends of the bridge were crowded and nearly every soldier had brought his family or his best girl. The guards found it hard to draw the line. I was a Mormon myself and came with two sweethearts.

Sam Mapes from up Rouge river came with his wife and family. Sam had the countersign but it did not pass the mother and squad of young recruits. He was, however, equipped with canteen and haversack and being the champion forager of Company B, 21st Michigan, he fed up and came back with rations for five days—some bits of everything on the tables except beans, including a roast pig that had not been carved and a hat full of cookies. I was not so slow myself and with my sweethearts had a dinner, seated on the grass in Hovey's grove. This homecoming was long remembered by the soldiers of the Civil war and by the citizens who planned and conducted it. I always thought those soldier boys paid more attention to the happy, daintily dressed waiters at the tables than they did to the pie that mother made. Fellows of my company surrendered unconditionally. The tables cleared away the couples tried to dance on the rough roadway. They found more pleasure talking to the moon that lighted Hovey's grove.

County Fair

In the year 1849 the farmers west of the village of Grand Rapids, made an exhibit of their products in an abandoned cornfield near the west end of Bridge-st. bridge. The ground is now occupied by the street railway barns. This affair was a success, and the farmers under the direction of Samuel Westlake of Walker township, formed an association mainly for mutual service among the widely scattered settlers.

Mr. Westlake, a finely educated man who practiced what he preached, was a power in the valley and under his supervision, annual fairs followed.

People from both up and down the river came in boats and those away from the water, with their wagons and in the saddle or on foot.

Premiums amounting to thirty-one dollars were awarded. They were made up by donations dropped into a box on a table under the wide spreading branches of the Council Pine.

Some years later the court-house square, now Fulton-st. park, was used as the fair grounds. The court building made an exhibition hall for art—mostly patchwork quilts and bedspreads—and agriculture. The live stock was chained to the trees or tied to the fence.

I well remember this fair. There were boys' footraces, wrestling and jumping matches and ball games in which the captains chose sides, the village against the country boys.

In 1855, the block on the west side of Division-st., north of Wealthy, which had been farmed and was at the time used for pasture, was taken over for fair grounds. Sheds were built and entrance gates erected.

Division-st. was well graded and made a fine race track open to the public. Not much better racing has been put up than that which Barney Laraway and Sol Wright conducted every afternoon during the fair. A three-year-old with a barefoot boy astride a sheep pelt saddle, cheering his colt while switching him far back with his swinging hat, as he came streaking out of the dust, gave one more thrills than all the mile-a-minute races ever staged. Bets ran high and furious, but the races were on the square. There were no put-up jobs and no stop-watches. The colt that arrived first won.

We did not realize then that men and boys were training to ride a few years later with Custer and Sheridan, and that Morgan pure horses were being bred to mount the Second and Third Michigan cavalry. "Rienzi," Sheridan's famous horse of history, was one of six hundred other Morgans raised by country boys in Western Michigan.

Admittance to the fair grounds was twenty-five cents.

THE YESTERDAYS

Those who were short of the quarter could climb the fence, but could not escape the wizard oil man, the soap peddler, or the prize package man who gave a shoe box full of jewelry for a wildcat dollar. The hot dog man had not yet arrived in the community.

The furniture exhibit at this fair consisted mainly of rocking chairs and cradles, which had ready sale as wedding presents. Deacon Haldane exhibited a two-story four-post bed with a trundle bed beneath to be pulled out at night for the children. This bed was made by hand at the bench.

George Pullman, later of Pullman car fame, another fine workman, exhibited the Boston rocking chair. There are some of them in the city to this day. Mr. Pullman, like most men of the time, was always hard up but never refused to pay the groceryman in trade from his work bench.

The great event of the fair, the giving of premiums, came on the third day. About this time Squire Philander Tracey's cow did not come home for milking, and after considerable search he found her in the fair grounds wearing a blue ribbon.

George Pullman had collected the premium—three dollars. The scrap that followed caused as much excitement as the races. Bets ran about even as to whether the cow jumped the fence or came through the gate.

In the end, Squire Tracey led his cow home and George Pullman kept the premium. Being flush, everybody called on the cabinet maker for something on account. If there had been a railroad here at the time Pullman might have remained with us, but while working long hours with his back to the wall he may have had a vision of the city across the lake which impelled him onward.

The success of this Division-st. fair encouraged the purchasing of forty acres of ground just south of the city, Hall-st. being the north line in later years. Sheds and buildings were built and these in 1861 became the barracks for the Cantonment Anderson. The race track was turned into a drill ground for cavalry, infantry and artillery, but was put in order again after the war and used many years, developing into a West Michigan exposition and moved finally to Comstock Park.

OF GRAND RAPIDS

The Old Arcade

Perhaps no locality in town has so much in the way of bits of history, comedy and tragedy as the short cut between Pearl and Lyon-sts., known as the Arcade.

In the early days this was an alley leading from Grab Corners to Kent, but along in the sixties William T. Powers, who owned considerable property nearby, made it a business thoroughfare. Later when Grand Rapids became a typical lumbering town with everything booming, including the river, there were in the county two hundred and forty-six water reservoirs, and eighteen licensed rum holes in near proximity to the Arcade.

It seemed that all the awful thirsts of the valley came here to slake. Orators were being imported at considerable expense to counteract this evil when Mr. Powers, with open eyes and in face of protest and ridicule, sent a drill three hundred feet into the earth on his own property in the Arcade and opened up a flowing stream of pure cold water tinged with iron.

In a short time the well was called "Iron John". Only Mr. Powers ever knew what it cost, but it flowed day and night for many years and was the greatest temperance reformer in the valley. Hundreds paused there daily—the business man, log runner, lumberjack, newsboy, and wandering dog, all shared in the coolness of the Arcade and the blessing of Iron John. A treasured visitor for a season or two was a little one-legged bird. The newspaper offices of the day were all in the vicinity. Hall's book store on the Pearl-st. corner; and Leppig's, where one could get the best coffee in town, on the Lyon-st. corner.

But the Arcade had its shadows and Tom Traxler, one of the most faithful police on night patrol, could have told you the unhappy side. Many the stray boy that Tom's kind arms carried from sleep in the dark corners, many the old booze fighter he booted toward jail for safe keeping.

The entrance to Powers theater for stage people and all their baggage, was up a stairway in the Arcade. One sultry night when all the windows were open and noise of the underworld drifted from the basement saloons down the block and

THE YESTERDAYS

blended with the applause and gay music in the theater above, Tom Traxler flashed his light into the foot of a dark stairway and staggered to Iron John, a moment later carrying a poor girl with a baby hugged in her arms. It was too late to save the mother, but kind hearted chorus girls gathering around seemed to understand and they cared for the baby.

In contrast to this undercurrent there was a great deal of neighboring and friendliness among the various business concerns along the block. This can best be told with this true story of a little dog.

Music was the name of the little beagle hound which used to wander up and down the streets around Grab Corners and in the Arcade along in the seventies. He would watch his chance to get in the door of Fred Loetgert's dry goods store and crawl into the waste-basket in Eliza Hall's millinery department, which was in the back of the store. This basket was beside Julie, deservedly the most popular saleslady thereabout for she had a kind word and open hand for every stray thing that drifted by. Music was all right until he got to snoring and then he became a nuisance and when Julie got tired of having him around she opened the door and told him to go bother his master at the Eagle office. One day she sent him forth with the following jingle tied to his neck by a piece of blue ribbon:

> I belong to Aaron T.,
>   But he don't care a cent for me.
> I wander up and down the street,
>   Sniff at every one I meet.
>
> Through the dust and mud I wade,
>   Part the time in the Arcade,
> Then in Leppig's stop awhile
>   To see Leppig's happy smile.
>
> Then from there across the way
>   With Charlie Hall to have a play
> Back again to Loetgert's shop,
>   There I have a happy lot.

Meat and crackers every day,
  Not a single cent to pay.
Julie gives them all to me—
  Happy may she ever be.

When some day I go to sleep
  In the basket at her feet
She'll forget to wake me up,
  Then goodby to this old pup.

Music went over to the Eagle office with this card attached to his neck and someone took it off and printed it in the evening paper under the heading of "Doggerel." So here in memory is just a bit of the shadow and sunshine of the old Arcade.

Tramps, After the War

For many years after the Civil war, the country including Western Michigan, was infested with hundreds of wandering men who roamed the continent over, sleeping any place at all and living on back door lunches and on the sympathies of the public, until patience was exhausted and stringent measures were taken to eliminate their kind.

Many have the impression that tramps were mainly men who had been in army service. This was true of some because for years after the war the totally disabled man received only eight dollars a month pension, and from that sum down to one dollar for lesser disabilities. These men found it difficult to adjust themselves and were often obliged to beg clothing and food. After the soldiers' homes were established there were few soldiers tramping.

The term "tramp" was not in use previous to the Civil war. It was army slang applied to troops on the march. Straggler was the term used to define a foot-loose man prowling about the country, and a majority of the service men who became tramps were stragglers in the army. Thus right after the war, it was easy enough to get a kitchen door hand-out by answering, "sure I was," to the query, "were you in the army?" People were imposed upon to such an extent that ultimately they refused these appeals and the tramps began placing a chalk mark code on walk or fence to indicate where one might receive hospitality. Householders, if in doubt regarding the wanderers deserving help, stipulated some service in return, such as splitting a bit of wood for the stove, only the ax frequently disappeared with the departing guest.

One dear old friend of mine, not liking to let a tramp in the house, sent him to the wood-shed with a sandwich and to put on a pair of her husband's cast-off shoes. Later she discovered one leg of a fine turkey, which had been hanging in store for Thanksgiving, had gone over the hill with the sandwich.

Of the men in my regiment I recall but one man who became a tramp. His ancestry, not his military life, was responsible. Half his father's law practice was in keeping him out of jail. He had the address of every man in the Twenty-first and called on them all on various pretexts. The last call he made on me was for a quarter to buy whitewash for a chicken coop. Next day I was called to police court to help get a friend out of town.

One well-educated soldier of my acquaintance never recovered from the wanderlust. I do not know where he found the girl he married, but they nailed the windows of a good farmhouse and gypsied forty years, traveling all over America. In the Yellowstone park they cooked for the tourists and slept under their wagon, with their dogs snarling in fright at the bears hunting garbage.

In these stirring days when Horace Greeley urged, "Go west, young man," thousands followed his advice and without a dollar drifted on over a trail blazed with chalk. To this flotsam was gradually added an army of hoboes, the latter the tin-can artists so much cartooned. They followed the railway and when thrown from the bumpers took revenge by wrecking the next train to come through in the night.

It took many years for the courts to discover that a job behind the bars of a workhouse would rid the country of tramps, also the three S's—soap, swatter and soup—were an eliminating factor. In some districts where they used the paddle first, the hobo did not wait for the soup.

In the winter the tramp had a hard time. Many a farmer's barn was fired by an old pipe, and in the town the saloon was often the only shelter. For several years there was a tramp's lodging house on Canal-st., now lower Monroe, where for five cents a man could have two by six feet on the floor, and for a dime, a blanket on a side wall plank. Often on blizzardly nights men were turned away; no room left. To get the shelter of the lockup tourists must commit some sort of crime. So mother's wandering Willie had a hard road to travel. Not till the supply of whisky was limited and a job breaking stone provided, did the army of tramps disband.

The First Railway Strike

In March, 1858, there was on West Bridge-st., where the Lake Shore freight house now stands, a rough riverstone building which for some time had been known as the "stone" grocery.

For some years this tippling grocery gave the last chance to buy wet goods on the way out of town. The brand of the whisky was labeled "Tommyhawk" and was drawn from the barrel into tin cups because the ordinary drinking glass was so easily broken when thrown against the stone wall above the shelves, which often held as much as one hundred dollars worth of groceries, including dozens of clay pipes at a penny each.

After passing Turner-av., Bridge-st. for three blocks sloped down grade to the level of an ancient river bed, then returned to higher ground. This low land was flooded at every river freshet and before a high sidewalk was built on the south line of the street, boys ferried people across in canoes for a two-cent piece.

This sidewalk had its perils. One night the best doctor in the town, who also was the alderman of the ward, in responding to a call, landed on his head in the mud. Then the city marshal attached a hand rail to guide men who had a filling of "Tommyhawk," as well as doctors and other night prowlers.

THE YESTERDAYS

In March, 1858, work was started on the grade of the Grand Rapids & Indiana railway just north of the stone grocery. The occasion was of great importance to the public and crowds assembled to watch the gang of shovelers. And here a few days later was staged the first strike in Grand Rapids.

When it had ended it is doubtful if the laborers could recall what caused it—too much Tommyhawk in the vicinity perhaps. Men lost their heads, or if not lost they were sold for a drink to walking delegates and the riot that followed called out the sheriff, who was a full sized man, but when he read the riot law to the gang they at once attacked him with picks and shovels.

With his back to the wall of the stone grocery, he fought single handed until a man with a long handled pitchfork began spearing him in the ribs. Then he used his revolver on the leader and when John Burke went down the gang scattered in a hurry. The coroner sat on John Burke and said it served him right. The grocery held a wake that lasted three nights, then business was resumed on the grade.

For a time timid people living in the west section went back and forth by way of Fourth-st., the next crossing to the north.

I do not recall what became of the building, but not long ago I saw a man on a Bridge-st. car smoking one of those clay pipes. The stem was worn short, but the odor was unmistakably that of the stone grocery.

Anson L. Norton was the name of that sheriff and for a time he was the hero of the town. He was re-elected to office. Then the Civil war called and he organized and became captain of the Michigan company which formed a part of the Lincoln cavalry regiment, Carl Schurz of New York was its first and Gen. A. T. McReynolds of Grand Rapids its second colonel.

An Old-Time Doctor

In the fifties there lived on the west side Dr. Blumrich, a German, large, portly and with a heart so big he could not get his coat to button.

Day or night was never so cold or dark that he failed to

respond to the call of the sick. Many were the stories told of his kindness and one comes to my memory as I think of those early days. In a modest home lived an old mother who did dressmaking to keep a bone in the cupboard for the dog, her only companion. When she fell sick with a misery in her back the good doctor came twice a day for a long time. It was a fight for life and they won, but the old woman was much worried over payment for Dr. Blumrich's services.

Said the doctor: "You will find my bill in the Bible on the table." So when the doctor was out of sight she crept from bed and in the good book found a ten-dollar bill.

The old doctor also spoke to Farmer Westlake on the Walker road and he left a load of four-foot maple, and to the boys, who made a bee and with their buck-saws and axes cut, split and piled the wood in the shed.

A neighbor woman who had a houseful of girls, but no boys, sent word that when the boys were through she would give them a feed of biscuit and honey. She did not know a hungry boy's capacity. They finished a tub of wild honey lately taken from a bee tree and plate after plate of biscuit.

In the party was a red-headed boy who seldom washed his neck and never combed his hair. He got an overdose of honey inside and much smeared on the outside. Before the next morning the doctor had been called to administer a dose of castor oil and collect fifty cents. Help for two others cost a dose of boneset tea and a dollar. Bless the doctor! He knew when it was right to take the butter for his bread.

When the old doctor passed into the country of the "beautiful somewhere" the entire community mourned him. The day of the funeral all business ceased. A German band led the long concourse to Greenwood—then much farther out in the country than it is today.

The band started from the church with customary dirge, slow and solemn, followed by all the fraternal societies of the town on foot, then a hundred vehicles. Any person who has marched to a dirge knows how difficult it is to keep the step, but away out Bridge and Stocking streets, over ungraded roads deep with ruts and dust and not until inside the cemetery did the band miss a note. It was a test of endurance for those who marched and those who played. There was no record of the time made, for in those days a trip to the cemetery was a solemn, dignified and sorrowful affair.

On the return the band usually played a quick step, but this time the horn players' lips were so stiff they could not blow a note. It was a day never forgotten by those who took part.

That was only one of numerous records made by that German band. The players put their whole soul into the notes without a thought of double pay for overtime. And the good old doctors, father, nurse and counselor to half the country round about, God bless them!

Surgery at the Shipyard Forge

About the year 1854 the east side of Canal-st. north of Lyon was built up with small frame stores as far as Bronson-st.—now Crescent-st. Back of the stores was an alley. All the buildings were set on piles well above the street grade. Where the National Biscuit Co. and other Bond-av. buildings now stand was a pond that was the happy home of the pollywogs, flies and mosquitoes; also fever and ague. I do not remember exploring this pond north of Bronson-st., for the boys of that region were hostile to the boys of Shantytown. On the east the pond met the hill.

In the summer there was usually about three feet of water on a ten-foot foundation of mud. Nobody had time to dig a ditch or this pond might have been drained into the river. Besides it made a good place to throw garbage.

Near the corner of Lyon and Canal-sts. was a grocery kept by a man and his wife. Often men went there for cracker and cheese lunches which they ate on the sidewalk because it was the more sanitary place.

One evening the stage brought in a capitalist from the east who had a carpet sack said to contain money that he was going to invest in town lots and pine lands. He must have inherited or borrowed this money, for he bore all the marks of a man of leisure, including a silk hat and white starched shirt with collar and cuffs. He took a look at the town and in his ramblings came into the shipyard forge. While he was there the cracker and cheese merchant and his wife indulged in their daily pasttime of family dispute. To the men working in the forge this was such a common and fifty-fifty affair that it attracted no attention, but the capitalist could not see a man beating a woman and listen to her screams without a protest. So he ran across to the store, caught the man by the collar and in an instant they were clinched.

The moment the woman was free she ran for the cheese knife and watching her chance slashed the man who dared interfere in their domestic affairs. After the first slash in the back the capitalist ran for the alley door with the woman in close pursuit and jumped the fence into the pond. He came out on the far side a plaster of mud. The woman's skirts held her back so she did not get a second slash at him as he ran for the forge, leaving a trail of eastern blood all the way.

The blacksmith laid him face down on a bench and someone hurried out for a doctor. The first one to arrive was Dr. DeCamp, who a few years later became famous as an army surgeon in the Civil war. It was his first big job and he had few instruments and no needles in his outfit; so the harness maker came running with a three-sided needle and a black linen thread.

It was much like stitching a patch on the seat of a man's trousers. Chloroform and microbes had not come into general circulation, but with liberal use of court-plaster and bandages the patient survived, though his groans brought in a shop full of spectators.

A few days later the capitalist bought a new suit of clothing at Julius Houseman's, paid the doctor and hotel bill and that is all this growing city attained of his wealth, so much needed at that time. He might have been sold a salt well if not for the interruption.

But trade at the cheese counter was great. All the men in town wanted a look at the woman and the more valiant of the women a glimpse at the knife she used on the peacemaker in the silk hat.

THE YESTERDAYS

The Sons of Malta

Grand Rapids had an organized Masonic lodge as early as 1844 and three by 1856. The Odd Fellows were well established by 1858. In 1859 there was organized in the village of Grand Rapids a secret society called the Sons of Malta.

The order was understood to claim origin in the Isle of Malta, but the resident branch seems to have drifted into somewhat convivial mood and was the source of much jollity and fun. The initiation fee was a keg of beer and when a man became a member he at once busied himself to further increase the membership of the lodge.

Led one evening by a German brass band under the leadership of Franz Blasle, the Sons of Malta came out on parade disguised much like dismounted Ku Klux. A pillow-case over the head and a bed sheet about the body completed the ghostly apparel. Some folk then had no change of sheets and the wives had to wait until their gay husbands came home before they could go to bed.

The ceremonies of initiation were mostly tricks of deviltry such as only real live wires could invent. Then, as now, men had confidence in their wives, and women, as today, did not forget a good story. The newspapers did not concern themselves with society columns and intimate news was distributed mainly through the sewing societies, which became an absolute necessity. The Malta lodge meetings were held Tuesday nights in a hall on Canal-st. The sewing circles met the next day. The lodge had a tough time trying to keep its affairs away from the public.

One night a high-headed candidate, thought he was being made too much of a target, and when he had cleaned up the hall it looked as though a cyclone had passed that way.

The members had so much to explain upon return to their homes that they became discouraged. Nearly every one had to account for black eyes, scalp wounds, barked skins, and torn shirts.

There were no assets since the initiation fee had been absorbed before the candidate came up for initiation and from that time the Sons of Malta seemed to have vanished like a fog before a gale.

When Simeon Baldwin Killed the Bear

In 1854 Simeon Baldwin had a brickyard at the "Forks of the Road," where the aristocratic Lake-dr. and Fulton-st. now meet. That part of the town was then mostly woods, scrub oak and frog ponds.

One day while Mr. Baldwin was shoveling clay from a pit into a mixer something came between him and the sun. Looking up he met the open mouth grin of a big black bear, who gave a sort of salute, raising on his hind legs and making the high sign with his paws, saying "woof," which translated meant "howdy." He only wanted to be a good neighbor, but Baldwin misunderstood "the bear who walked like a man" and he cast the shovel away and made fast time to his cabin.

The wild brother of the woods thought no doubt that was the white man's invitation to dinner and ran a close second, saying "woof, woof" at every jump. If it had been a longer distance he would have been in the lead at the cabin door. All the time there was running through the brickmaker's mind the then popular song, "Johnnie, get your gun, get your gun." The gun was hanging near the door, loaded with buckshot for blue racers that abounded in that vicinity and sometimes played tag with the boys when they went to drive the cows home in the evening. The first shot finished the bear and nearly kicked Baldwin into the next lot.

The following day the bear skin was hanging outside a store on Monroe-st. The meat, dressed, weighed three hundred and twenty-four pounds and found a ready sale.

Bear meat is not unlike pork and dad brought home a roast, but somehow I could not eat it. I felt sorry for the brother of the woods who in a spirit of friendliness had lost out and became a party to a skin game.

The bear's fat was made into oil. Mixed with alcohol and scented with bergamot it was quite a popular hair dressing for men of early days.

I never did take kindly to hair oil, for mother made us wear night caps if we oiled our heads and only girls wore night caps.

About that time William Haldane used to hang out at the shipyard forge. He came in with a loaf of bread and a bear steak to make his noon lunch. He was one of the men who never had a grouch. As he broiled his meat on an iron rod over the coal fire, he told us his bear story.

It was in 1837 that he made his first visit to the Rapids, coming from Ohio in a single horse and buggy. Beyond Flat river he met in the road a fine black dog—a very welcome sight as he had driven many miles without seeing a house, and a dog was a sure sign of a settlement.

So he got out of the buggy to cultivate closer acquaintance. The animal disputed the right of way and when he went after it with a club, clambered up a tree, sat on a limb and grinned at him. Down in Ohio dogs did not climb trees. So Haldane was anxious to own this one and he took one of the driving lines, made noose in the end and climbed up in the tree. He got the noose over the animal's head and lowered him to the buggy, but there he made so much trouble that he finally chucked it into an empty feed bag. This took much time and it was after dark when Mr. Haldane arrived at Mr. Fisk's house at the mouth of the Thornapple river.

At the stable he found a piece of rope and fastening it about the neck, dragged the animal into the house, where it ran under a bed.

Mrs. Fisk liked dogs, but objected to sleeping with a bear in the room, so at bedtime she and her husband climbed the ladder into the attic and pulled the ladder up after them.

Mr. Haldane succeeded in bringing the young bear to the Rapids, where it became the playmate of all the children in the neighborhood.

The Tale of Three Bears

In Baxter's history of Grand Rapids he tells of three bears that came to town as late as 1870.

The people of that time were much the same as those of today. They put the large berries on the top of the box and Mr. Baxter at the time of his writing simply put the large berries at the top, but I will endeavor to fill in below with what happened to the bears after they came to town.

There was a circus in town on Waterloo (Grandville) street hill. In those days there were no billboards to disfigure the landscape and every farmer's barn for miles around was plastered with circus bills. This gayety along with the failure of the blackberry crop, no doubt induced the three bears—a mother and two well grown cubs—to come in by way of Walker-av. and Seventh-st. to the river.

As the water was low and to avoid paying toll on the bridge the bears crossed on the dam with all the small boys who had not been able to "git to go" to the circus following at a respectful distance. Bears know a lot more than they are given credit for and like other fellows who live in the country these bears stopped to look at the skyscrapers and other wild things along upper Canal-st. There were some things on the street then that were very wild.

This sightseeing was a trifle indiscreet on the part of the bears, for it gave the people time to arm against the invaders and make their way around by Bridge-st. bridge. There was an ordinance prohibiting shooting in the city, but from all about came men and boys with every conceivable weapon from corn cutters to spades and pitchforks. The bears evidently got the scent of one sauerkraut chopper—and quickly made their way up the hill where they stopped for a few social calls before vanishing in the oak grubs beyond.

It is recorded that they played tag with a pig or two in the streets and tipped over a beehive while the owner thereof gathered her petticoats and climbed a ladder to the wood-shed roof and they left the locality in such a fever of excitement that for several days people locked their doors and slept with carving knives near at hand.

But this anxiety was needless, for all the time the bears were feeding on sweet apples in Gaylord Holt's orchard on the Thornapple river. Mr. Holt had a variety of sweet apples that was known far and wide to bears and boys. When they combined their appetites the grower got about as many as he could carry in his pockets.

THE YESTERDAYS

The section of the city that was inspected by the bears went through many thrilling events but none its folk liked to talk about more often. For the next ten years people dated their coming to the Rapids by the year the three bears crossed the river on the dam.

Squire's Opera House and "Uncle Tom"

Historians date the first bloodshed of the Civil war at Fort Sumter. No one has recorded the trail of gore that followed the "Uncle Tom's Cabin" theatricals over our northern land. The story of Uncle Tom was like kindling applied beneath a cauldron already steaming hot.

People who lived in Grand Rapids about 1859 remember Squire's opera house, located on the west side of Canal-st. not far from Bridge, and some may have cause to remember the full week's engagement of an Uncle Tom troupe of actors from way down east.

They came in by stage and with their arrival came a story that the bloodhounds had captured and eaten a runaway Negro at Kalamazoo.

My excuse for writing this comes from the fact that I had the job of distributing the handbills on the street and helping on the stage in the evening at fifty cents per day. It was good summer-time work and fine work for a boy—like digging gold and acquiring a liberal education at the same time.

Uncle Tom, Eliza, Topsy, Simon Legree, and Marks the lawyer, were stars. Topsy, I soon learned, was an alley boy in his home town. His only makeup was a woolly wig, some burnt cork and a gunny-sack dress. Nature had provided him the "makeup"—a girlish form with the ugliest pair of soup bone shins. With his dancing and "nigger" shines he was enough for a full show. Behind the curtain Legree and Uncle Tom were good friends, but in the parts on the stage friendship was forgotten. The audience that packed the house, already disturbed and partisan over the slavery agitations of the day, were carried away with the story. They wept over little Eva, mourned for Uncle Tom and wiped their eyes for poor

Eliza. They hissed Legree and somebody threw a cat at Lawyer Marks.

The rear of the opera house opened on an alley that bordered the canal. Beyond was the river. In summer all male members of show companies washed up in the canal and when the stage hands with Topsy and Legree, each with a cake of soap and a towel, came out in the light of the lanterns that were hanging at the door, they were welcomed by a gang of Shantytown boys. These informed Legree that Grand Rapids was no place for a nigger driver and they started to put him in the swim for Grand Haven.

Legree got his back to the wall and if there had been more light than from a single hanging lantern what happened might better not be told. But I noticed that when Legree failed to ring the bell Topsy pulled the wire. Those Shantytown boys had no chance to clinch and the pile driver blows knocked them off the narrow path into the canal, where some of them were glad to wash the stars out of their heads.

When the battle had ended, Topsy had lost his gunny sack. His white body with a black face was funnier than his make-up on the stage.

The next evening the curtain rolled up before an overflow audience. From the center of the stage hung a punching bag and Legree came out and in a pleasant way said:

"It is the duty of an actor to give the best there is in him," and added that the events of the evening before had given him assurance that his part had been well taken. He laid aside his coat and stripped to the waist, gave them an exhibition of a boxing master's skill. Then thanking the young gentlemen who attended the social of the previous evening the show proceeded before a somewhat chastened crowd of spectators.

The First Strawberry Farm

There is an interesting story regarding the first cultivation of the strawberry in the valley of the Grand, or at least in the first commercial patch of the delicious fruit.

Once upon a time, way back east, there was a village

THE YESTERDAYS

boy who like all boys had an appetite. During June days he was chased out of every field of meadow land for miles about where strawberries grew wild in the grass. Farmers said he trampled down the hay. So intent was he down on his knees trying to fill his little basket that often the owner of the meadow caught him by the neck of his shirt and sent him over the rail fence into the road. It seemed to him there was no place where he could get a basketful without disaster overtaking him in the search.

But he was encouraged by a neighbor's girl who told him to go west and find a patch he could call his own and she would come and help pick them. So when he was twenty-one he packed all his property in a carpet sack and hiked to the Grand river country. Several miles below the Rapids he found the ideal place where a few acres had been cleared by the Indians and planted for years in corn. He bought out the red man and planted in rows the strawberry plants taken from the fields along the river bank. All about were masses of wild plums, crabapples, thornapples, blackberries, gooseberries and grapes. The white men came that way and said, "Stedman, you are a blank fool." But Stedman, an aggressive man with a fist as large as a boxing mitt, told them to go to.

The wild berry, unlike the wild Indian, grew under cultivation. The upriver town grew also and boys and girls came down in canoes and picked on shares.

The grower's half was sold in town, the picker's share made shortcakes. Stedman's girl came from the east and joined him and while the berry patch grew the crop of children forced an addition to the house.

It was about this time the writer came into the game. He had a large canoe that would carry three girls and their baskets and all through the berry season he made daily trips.

One of the stolen pleasures of those trips was a visit to a swimming hole on the far side of a willow-covered sand bar while the girls toiled on. The idea that girls would like to go where they could get wet all over at once, had never entered the minds of people.

After many years Mr. Stedman came to my father and

said, "Jim, I've made some money and have a lot of children. I am going across the lake and spread out on a prairie farm where I can raise cattle and sheep. Everybody is raising strawberries now. They have found out how good they are. I only went into the business anyway to spite those hide-bound hayseeds back east." So he went away from the river farm where it is said the first cultivated strawberries in the Grand river valley were grown.

There are folks now who claim the wild berry has a better flavor than the tame one. I wonder were they ever chased out of the meadow by a farmer and his dog? There is an old saying: "That doubtless, God could have made a better berry, but is doubtful if he ever did."

The Shingle Maker

One of the industries of the early days which is now almost forgotten, was the making or shaving of shingles. The shingle weaver, so called from the way he wove and bound the shingles into bundles, was an important factor in the development of Western Michigan.

The first settlers were wasters of timber and the great pines were ruthlessly cut down for the first cuts of clear stuff. What would not split into shingles was left to decay or burn, being considered too light for good stove wood.

The great pine was really the despair of the pioneer, for aside from the shingle it was hard to dispose of, it being almost impossible to burn the stumps. They simply charred over. But in making shingles the settler found means by which to live while clearing the land and raising a crop.

One of these shingle weavers whom it was my privilege to know was Nicholas Emmons. He came from the east and was one of the first men to settle on the shores of Camp lake, near Sparta. To reach this promised land of the west and make a home for his wife and two sons he walked several hundred miles with a pack upon his back. This may seem a simple matter in this day of good roads and with every convenience along the way, but I cannot adequately express what it meant at that time. As one man after another passed through the settlements to be swallowed up by the forests one only knew that there was no wild life to ambush him. His powers of endurance were the test. He was not unlike the birds of the air in their flights each season. There was some power that impelled him onward.

When Emmons arrived at Camp lake there were only a few scattered settlers with their little log cabins and mere patches of cleared land. With a ten-foot pole he surveyed his quarter-section in the great forest and built his cabin of logs, with its stone and mud fireplace, facing on the water. When all was ready he went back east for his wife and boys. How often have I sat before the fire in that little loghouse and feasted on new maple syrup and dear Mother Emmons' biscuit and fritters, for my father and mother lived only a mile from them for four years after the Civil war.

The Emmons' had been there twenty years at that time but had never gotten through cutting shingles. A bunch of shingles was legal tender, as good as a bank account when starvation was a window peeper and the cold winds of winter whistled through the elbows of a worn-out coat.

To pull one end of a cross-cut saw with Uncle Nick Emmons and turn the great pine into shingles, chop, split, rive and shave, then pack until there was load enough for an ox team, then sixteen miles over the forest trail to the Rapids!

It took all of a week's time to make a load of shingles and get to town and back, but it meant provisions, spelling books for boys, wool cloth for a pair of pants, so dad's old ones could be made over for son, and perhaps a bit of something for mother. Shingles covered the cost of the absolute necessities until the land was cleared and crops at hand. We recall the hard times and wildcat money of the town people, but they always found enough to get to the circus. The weaver's dollar was often as large as his cabin. I class these men as the real pioneers of Western Michigan, but their only monuments are a few pine stumps, black ghosts of the forests. Their shingles floated away from the Rapids on the lumber rafts and river boats, they traveled to every part of the country by water and rail, they sheltered the rich and the poor, covered the mansion and the cowshed. Personally the ones I remember most clearly were those that in the hands of the school ma'am landed upon my spanker beam.

The Islands

Although the Rapids was a good sized town when I came here, the islands were still in the river, and known only by number as one, two, and three. There was a fourth, about which there was a dispute. French people called it Robard's, others Robarge, but it was of little importance. The three formed a beautiful river park that had it been retained in its primitive grandeur, could not have been surpassed by any work of man.

I had a love for islands, because my great adventure before coming to Michigan was when my father put me in the bow of a canoe and paddled to Butternut island in the St. Lawrence river, where we camped out and gathered a load of hazel and butternuts for the coming winter. From that time islands had a grip on me that I made no effort to cast off.

The number one island began just about the foot of Lyon-st. and number three terminated about where the Wealthy-st. bridge now crosses the river. The three islands were divided by narrow channels and rapid currents. Only small boats could navigate between.

My first view was in June, 1854, when from the top deck of the river steamer we came up the east channel to land at the Eagle hotel dock. A few days later I was getting acquainted with the town and near the Butterworth foundry met Harry Eaton and his gang, who by way of initiation to the west, proceeded to push me off a slab pile into the river to see if I could swim. I could and struck out for the head of Island number one.

A few Indian wigwams were under the wide branching maple trees which gave protection from sun and rain, and two laughing Indian boys in canoes were trying to capsize each other. A solitary Indian standing like a statue under a tree grunted his disapproval of the boys on the shore and disappeared into his tepee.

THE YESTERDAYS

Sitting on a rock in the sun to dry my clothing, I studied the rapids and hundreds of large boulders of granite and lime rock about which the waters rushed. Except for a little cleared land where the Indians had planted corn, the west shore was all a meadow of deep, rich grass and blended tints of wild growth.

In after years I often thanked Harry Eaton for pushing me off that slab pile, because it gave me my first day under those wonderful water maples. I was somewhat older before I really appreciated the great sycamores at the water's edge, the island plateau of giant water elms, the almost tropical mass of grape vine that festooned the trees, and in every depression the wild plum and crabapple that crowded the elder bushes and sumac, and that I came to love the tinkle of bells, on cows that had waded the river to feed on the abundant grass, blended with the music of blackbirds and bob-o-links swaying about on the cattails.

On the east channel, nearly opposite the foot of Pearl-st., stood the great-grandfather of all sycamores, just above the low water mark. When the Indians set up their wigwams there in the spring they suspended swings for the children on the long angling branches, and hung baskets of food far out on the limbs away from the reach of dogs. In the white man's day many boats were locked to staples driven in the body of this tree.

But even then the three islands were almost without a blemish. Indians never built a fire at the foot of a tree and the high water that flooded the islands each year washed them free of all refuse of their camps. The heavy covering of grass and plants prevented washing of the soil. The prevailing west winds wafted the odors of trees and flowers over the village.

May not an old man of today be forgiven for a longing that this beautiful playground of his boyhood might have been spared for his great-grandchildren? Only men of deep thinking can tell you how long nature was in creating and clothing these islands, but any school boy with a piece of chalk can figure how long man was in obliterating the last trace of them.

The Mission Land

French Jesuit missionaries located headquarters at Mackinac Island prior to 1662. From there members were sent to all the Indian tribes along Lake Michigan, including Grand river, more than two hundred years ago, but nothing very definite has been learned from their records.

By the treaty with the Indians of the Grand river valley in 1821, among other concessions, was one square mile of land for mission purposes. Beside the river well-worn trails led to this location which was staked to run south and west from the present corner of West Bridge and Front-av. There is little in print that gives personal touch with the men who selected the location, but they were wise beyond our thoughts today. Besides being sacred to the Indian as the land of his ancestors, the birthplace of his traditions; the scenic beauty of forest and stream, its abundance of fruit, game and fish had attracted the Indian for unknown ages to this place.

When the first missionaries had established their log schoolhouse, church and blacksmith shop they saw at once that some day it would become a place of importance. Others saw this as well; the trader quick to take advantage of the furs which the Indian would trap, the speculator with an eye to the forests of valuable trees and more important than either, the settler who would populate the country with an enterprising white race.

As a place where the Indian would be civilized the mission was a dismal failure and by the terms of the treaty the lands were eventually sold and the proceeds divided, the Baptists receiving $12,000 and the Catholics $8,000 after a long period of litigation. The old buildings were not totally obliterated until the early sixties.

In the fifties the land was platted. A dense growth of oak grubs covered most of the ground except where the Indians and a few whites had grown corn and other crops.

Boston capitalists secured the land and gave to the streets

THE YESTERDAYS

very generally the names of popular Boston avenues, having no sentiment and little thought of its becoming historic ground. There was no one to say a good word for the red man who used such poetical and appropriate terms for every locality. I know of no place in western Michigan of its size with so much hidden history, tradition, myth and romance buried beneath its busy life of home and factory.

The three buildings of the mission are well remembered by the people of the fifties. They were by that time weather beaten shacks, windowless and mere wind breaks for the cattle that pastured on the commons. The beautiful bronze plate placed by the D. A. R. on the street car barns on Front-av. does not mark the exact location of the buildings but is as near as can be and remain permanent.

The riverstone forge of the deserted smithshop had a charm for small boys. It was an ideal place to roast green corn "cooned" from garden patches.

One day there came to work in father's shop, Burritt, one of the early mission blacksmiths. He had lived most of his life among the Indians and they came from long distances to get his help in repairing their guns and spears. He often joined the boys at the old mission forge and they became very fond of him.

One day two Indians came in a Mackinaw boat and talked a long time in the Ottawa dialect with Burritt. After they had gone he told father he was lonely and was going back to the reservation at Pentwater because the Indians needed him. Father said he was the best missionary the Ottawas ever had. When Burritt took the final trail to the happy hunting ground all the Indians on the reservation were there to listen to the farewell tribute of an Indian preacher, given in his own impressive way.

Personally I had no acquaintance with or recollection of any of the early missionaries, but know that Chief Noon Day of the Ottawas was the most prominent convert to the white man's faith.

OF GRAND RAPIDS

Rafting and the Chanty Men

Before and for some time after the coming of the railroads all the lumber made in the Grand Rapids valley, that was not used to supply the local demand, was rafted to the Haven, where it was loaded on ships for other lake ports. The boats were usually two or three-masted schooners manned by hardy sailors, whose skill brought them into port through narrow channels in gales of wind and often driving snow.

There were many sawmills on Grand river and its tributaries that had no other shipping facilities. Logs from the nearby forests came in on the snow, on sleds, and were rolled into the booms and ponds of the water-power mills, sawed to dimension and then in the quiet water made into rafts by men skilled in the business. First came long, heavy stuff for a foundation, then shorter lumber for cross piling. By a system of overlapping or shingling, the lumber was woven into many layers. In times of good water the rafts were two feet thick. Heavy pieces at the top were pinned at the ends and to the bottom sills, with tough hardwood split from river bank trees. All the tools needed were an ax and an auger. When the raft was finished there was often added a deck-load of shingles and lath.

By reason of the chute in the dam at the rapids here these rafts could not be more than sixteen feet wide, but were often two hundred feet in length. A long, heavy sweep at either end for steering gear and then with a crew of five men the raft was ready to float.

Once out of the small streams the many rafts were made into fleets and floated to the quiet ponds above the dam at Grand Rapids, where again they were separated into single rafts in order to pass the chute and sent through the rapids to quiet water below. There they were again assembled for their final voyage to the Haven.

The great adventure was the passage over the dam and down the narrow chute and channel of the rapids and often in high water the rafts were wrecked against the boulders outside the channel or swept crosswise of the current, where they made a dam of themselves. One season a raft climbed the breakwater of Bridge-st. bridge and was torn to pieces. The raftsmen were seriously hurt and nearly drowned.

The salvaging of lath and shingles was a source of considerable profit to energetic boys who received five cents a bunch from the owners. Drift lumber furnished material for many of the farm buildings along the banks of the Grand. Stray boards, like stray thoughts, could not prove their owners and there were no claimants.

Rafting developed a new type of man. Almost any man could run a boat down stream, but it required a peculiar skill and river instinct to keep a long fleet of lumber rafts out of the way of passing river steamers, to avoid sand-bars and the lure of lost channels and bayous on the lower stretches where the wind was apt to struggle for the master hand.

The sweeps for the steering must work in unison and so the men sang or chanted as they worked.

The chanty man, as he has been called, had his beginning with what is perhaps the most beautiful work of man's hands —the sailing ship—and the "chantys" are the working songs of the water. Many of them have been handed down through generations and followed certain haunting melodies, but the songs of the raftsmen were usually improvised to suit the occasion. There was hardly a duty on the floating fleet of lumber which had not its own chanty to go with it, with one line solo and four lines chorus, in which all the events of the journey were told.

I suppose the voice of the average raftsman was on a low level, but one could not be insensible to the charm of the song and the swishing of the sweeps that came to one out of the night or from above some river bend.

That grand old river man, Thomas Friant, could tell you of chanty men who sang their way from the River Rouge to the lumber docks at the Haven.

Nearly all the raftsmen were French-Canadian. They worked in the lumber woods in the winter and drifted naturally to the river in the summer. Returning from the Haven to the Rapids by boat the rest of their journey to the mills was on foot. The returning trip always included a day in town and meals at the hotel. On the way down the river the captain bought supplies from the farms and they lived on the fat of the land.

Saddle Bag Swamp

When I was a boy in young Grand Rapids it was customary for the people to go out and gather the wild fruit for the table and for preserving for winter use, Saddle Bag swamp was the best place in all the valley for gathering the high bush huckleberry. This swamp was about six miles east of the city and there were two ways of getting there: By following the Rix Robinson trail or over a winding, sandy road—now East Leonard Street.

Ditches and drains have left but little evidence of this basin of water and rich black land, the last trace of an ancient lake bed. The first survey lines of the Detroit, Grand Haven & Milwaukee railroad crossed this territory, but the swamp hungrily swallowed the roadbed on several occasions and the men who built it were obliged to turn aside to the higher ground.

The swamp was free to everybody and barefoot boys with their baskets, farmers in their wagons, and the well-to-do in their buggies resorted there to gather berries. In the autumn it was a profitable place for the hunter. It was also the natural home for many rare wild flowers, the orchids, pink and yellow lady slippers and the pitcher plant, or fly trap, among them. Plant lovers who ventured there in the spring days wore hip wading boots—more as a protection against snakes than water, for everything in the line of wiggling serpents from the harmless little garter-snake to the black water-snake, rattler and blue racer might be encountered there.

I ventured into this swamp one frosty morning when on the ground under almost every clump of bushes was a coil of reptiles, chilled and numb with the cold. I went at that time for the high bush cranberries that were ripe and bordering the water pools with the glow of crimson fruit.

Not far from one border of the swamp lived a man who was trying to clear a farm and make a living and that man had a boy. The boy is now the gold braided, white haired policeman, John Conlon, who has tramped his beat on the streets of Grand Rapids nearly forty years. I will tell you as nearly as I can a story that he told me only a week or so ago.

"It was the day before the Fourth of July. There was to be a grand celebration in the Rapids, fireworks and a parade. I longed to go but what could a boy do in town on the Fourth without so much as one cent of money to spend and there was nothing in the house or on the farm to sell. But mother was my chum and she came forward with a basket and the suggestion that I go to the swamp and gather berries and perhaps I could find someone in town to buy them. I fought snakes and worked until dark, but I got enough ripe berries to fill the basket and my hat. At six o'clock Fourth of July morning I was trudging down Monroe-st. in my Sunday clothes, but barefoot and carrying my heavy basket.

"On the front steps of the National hotel—right over there where the Morton now stands—was the colored cook. He hailed me. 'Boy, what you all got in that er basket.' I showed him the berries and with a delighted grin he offered me a silver dollar. I followed him through to the kitchen and he chuckled all the way over the huckleberry pie his folks were going to get for their Fourth of July dinner.

"At that time there was a spring brook with its source at the foot of the hills. It came in a winding, careless way, across lots, then ran under the hotel porch into a sluice that crossed the street. I was hungry, hot and tired and I went out from the kitchen and knelt down by the brook and drank and washed the dust off my face. As we stood here today I can see that old National hotel with its white paint and green window blinds—and the brook running into its hiding place under the steps. And my silver dollar? Never did an American boy get quite so much for his hard earned money."

Saddle Bag swamp in the early days was considered almost worthless; in fact, the first settlers bought it up for something like a shilling an acre. As the country became cleared the owners set a tax of a few cents a quart for picking berries—

The Wild Pigeon

Among the most wonderful of bird stories is that of the wild pigeon. I am glad that there are still living many witnesses to the facts I am relating, for otherwise I might be charged with fairy tales.

At the time the first white man came to Michigan the woods were filled with flocks of these beautiful birds. They nested in trees, in a bundle of sticks and lived in pairs until September or October when they gathered in flocks for their flight to the South. Though many were killed each year they increased in numbers. I recall seeing them in flocks when on windy days they flew so low that they were often killed with cane fish poles or long sticks. They seemed to gather in flocks as by a general order and in their flight over the city, with the speed and almost the roar of an airship, they made great wing shooting.

A favorite stopping place with them was at the salt meadows below the west side plaster mills. The water there had a slightly salt taste, very agreeable to man, and seemed much liked by the birds. They fed also on the grass and on the oak ridges to the west. I have seen a hundred acres densely covered with flocks going and coming about these marshes.

As a food these pigeons were a great blessing to the early settlers. Through several winters my mother served spiced pigeon to her guests as a choice dish. In the cellar were rows of stone jars packed solid with birds pickled in spiced apple cider and sealed with air-tight covers. The minister never had to eat woodchuck at our house.

I am permitted to use the word of Frank Chickering, a long-time resident of this city, who followed pigeon netting as a business for several years. Mr. Chickering says:

"I learned to catch pigeons in a net when I was ten years old at Millford, N. H. When fourteen years old I went to Sandy Creek, N. Y., hired a horse and wagon and drove six miles to Boylston, where the birds were nesting and feeding.

THE YESTERDAYS

I made one haul and caught forty-two dozen and two pigeons.

"I hired people in the vicinity to pick them and shipped them by express to New York City, where I received four dollars per dozen. That was in 1856. For many years I followed the birds to their nesting and feeding places as far south as the Cumberland mountains and north to many points in Michigan.

"Their first nesting was in the south and their second in the north. Their nests in the trees were made of a few sticks to hold two eggs. The females left the nest at daylight to feed, going as far as twenty miles, and the males took their places. When the mother bird returned her mate went out, coming back at dark. They fed upon all kinds of nuts, the grass of lowland fields, and left the country entirely stripped of everything green.

"The nets were set in an open space, the operators concealing themselves in clumps of brush. The net was thrown by a spring pole. Decoy pigeons were staked out and a few handfuls of corn scattered in range of the net. Coming in flocks with the speed of the wind the birds swirled down about the decoys until the ground was blue with them. The spring pole threw the wide net and the birds were captives, their heads only coming up through the meshes in their efforts for liberty. Their heads were pinched to kill them. They were hauled away by wagon loads to the warehouse and prepared for shipment to New York and Boston markets.

"Many men followed the birds, netting them every year until 1880, when they disappeared and never since has a single one of them been seen."

Mr. Chickering says he will pay $1,000 for a pair of live birds and the National Geographic society has a standing offer of $5,000 for a pair.

I know that to the present generation the story of the pigeon may seem a romance so I take the opportunity to quote in brief from the writings of Audubon and Wilson, two of the greatest observers of bird life.

Audubon noticed "a continuous flight of pigeons for three days, to his calculation one billion, one hundred and fourteen million." As every bird consumed half a pint of food daily, figure it out yourself.

Wilson gives an account of a roosting place in the woods that occupied a large area. "The ground was covered several inches with their droppings, all the grass and underbrush destroyed, the surface strewn with large limbs broken down by the weight of birds and the trees for thousands of acres destroyed as if girdled with an ax. When these roosts were first discovered people came in the night and with clubs and other implements of destruction killed them by the wagon load. One of these breeding places was several miles in width and forty miles in length. In many trees more than one hundred nests were made."

These wonderful birds had but one enemy so far as we know and that was man. There was no closed season and followed so relentlessly from nesting to feeding place may it not be that the same instinct that controlled their flights guided them to some vast wilderness unknown to man?

The Straw Man

Along in the 1850's the mattress maker was still bunking in Noah's ark and the inventor of the spring bed had not been born.

Cords were the proper support for the billow of feathers or straw ticks that made up the bed. In our town as in every other, the rich slept in feathers and common folk on straw. One way in which to detect a rich man or woman was by the feathers in whiskers or hair, while the others, particularly the young men, reveled in wild oats. Wheat straw did not sprout so readily as oat and was cheaper.

Every good housekeeper filled her bed ticks with fresh straw one a month and mother for her spare bedroom would use nothing but the best oat that had been threshed by flails. One time father pulled a man out of the river and he was so grateful that when he threshed his oats he brought to our barn a full load of straw—enough to last a year. We carried out the ticks and filled up with oat straw until we had to use a chair to climb into bed. Next to the hickory shirts which

THE YESTERDAYS

men wore at that time the bed ticking was the meanest cloth made.

Most of the fresh bedding was purchased from peddlers who went about the streets with their wagons and horses shouting "straw, straw." In early morning the straw man's call waked all the babies and in some cases "straw" was the first word they learned to say. The straw man was the noisiest thing in town and became such an irritation to the nerves of the feather bed citizens that Charles Warrell, our city clerk, in desperation composed a poem about the straw man which was read to the city council and printed on the front page of the Daily Eagle. I do not know that the poem was made a part of the official proceedings, but it became the base of an ordinance that muzzled the straw man.

There appeared in the society news one July day an item to the effect that Mrs. Uptown, who was one of the "two-hundred," had substituted straw for her feather bed. The lady stopped her paper and her husband went fishing for a few days. Nowadays the reporter would have explained more tactfully that the lady had gone to the seashore during the heated season.

All good things come to an end and some fellow invented the wire springs and cotton mattress and the straw bed became a thing of the past.

There was still some use left for straw. It served on the floor as padding under the carpets and later until the recent dry spell, the large, smooth specimens were used by persons of discriminating taste in disposing of a concoction called a mint julep.

Pay Days

Commercial credit was good along in the fifties. There were two times for settlement of debts; in the spring when suckers were running and sheep being sheared, and after harvest when wheat was threshed.

With the moving out of the ice the suckers came up the river like rays of sunshine. They were legal tender for all transactions. A second bank had come to town and fishermen could put up a string of suckers as collateral for a loan, provided the borrower accepted the bank's "wildcats."

It must have been conditions here that gave Barnum the thrill that produced that epic, "There is a sucker born every minute." Grand river speeded up and produced a sucker every second. The inhabitants feasted on suckers. Fried with salt pork, boiled with cream and butter dressing, stuffed with dressing, the platter garnished with watercress and always a few barrels salted for winter consumption.

It was claimed that old residents became so expert they kept a run of suckers going in one corner and a bundle of neatly tied bones coming out the other corner of their mouths. And some of those old residents thought they ought to collect a royalty from McCormick, the inventor of the self-binding harvester. This idea came when he visited here a few days and witnessed our perpetual motion machine. One of our surgeons hung a sort of safety first card in his office: "Don't hurry. A bone in the mouth is worth two in the throat."

The wool growers had no time to net suckers. They sheared sheep to pay their store bills, then made logging bees to clean up more land for pasture. Everybody was invited, a sheep butchered for dinner and those "bees" became such a daily event that men claimed that wool began growing between their teeth. It was an act of Providence that made sheep produce twin lambs or there would not have been mutton to go around.

Thus the people swapped crops until the spring run of suckers came again. Of course there were many other fine food fish, but it was quantity production that counted. Many a pair of lovers spent blissful hours on the bridge watching the sturgeon and red fin mullet.

The fellow who goes casting for bass is a poet with an appetite and in those days one might often meet a man with the soul of a Tennyson dragging a six-foot sturgeon along the board walk of the main street.

The Salt Water Baths

A short distance north of Bridge-st. bridge on the east

river bank along in the forties was a large, barn-like structure, Truman H. Lyon's salt works. The building was over a deer lick spring, the water of which was brackish and indicated salt not far away. Wells were drilled and large wooden tanks in the basement held the water which was pumped for storage before reaching the evaporating process.

Considerable salt was made here, but financially the business was not a success so along in the fifties the building was remodeled into an edge tool factory, but the tanks were left in the basement, the overflow going into the river.

Charles Hathaway, the proprietor and chief workman, was a man well liked by all who knew him. A fact always interesting to boys was that his father was one of George Washington's generals in Revolutionary days.

In the factory were heavy trip hammers and forges where many kinds of edge tools of combined iron and steel were welded together by a flux of borax that flashed from the hammer blows in streams of liquid fire. The workmen wore leather aprons to protect themselves and the boys loved to hang around and watch them.

Mr. Hathaway told the boys about the water tanks in the basement. When the day's work was done the trap in the floor was raised and the men washed themselves free from the grime of the forge with a salt water bath and he gave the boys permission to play there when the place was not in use by the men.

Bathing suits were an unthought-of need then, and now when I visit the bathing beaches I am wondering if we are not getting back to those unblushing days.

The water was cold and frequently the fellows ran up the stairway to dress by the heat of the forge. It was not always by accident that some of them got a blister, for if they became too numerous a spurt of hot scales and borax shot out from some trip hammer, catching them amidships and sending them home with their soup bone shanks resembling a case of measles.

Sometimes if there were no people on the bridge walk near

by, they went from the salt water tank to the warmer water of the river.

This salt water bathing had a few drawbacks. The great timber supports of the basement became covered with a red rust that not even soft soap would wash out of a fellow's shirt. Nevertheless, it must have contributed some good red blood to the community, for among the men who played there as boys were Charles Leonard of refrigerator fame, Gaius Perkins, Sidney Stevens; Fred Church, the Artist; Le Grand Pierce, Charlie and Fred Rose; Del Squires, the acrobat; and Peter Weber and Charles Bolza, who went down on southern battlefields.

The pleasure of the salt baths became noised about and R. E. Butterworth, a wideawake man with shops at the foot of the canal, drilled a well and put in modest bathtubs for those who had a quarter to spare. The brine of the bathrooms was all right, but the common run of boys jumped or dived from the railroad bridge at the head of the rapids or to the west of the islands and the Butterworth mineral baths had to be discontinued for want of patronage.

In the meantime the gang increased at the tool factory and overflowed from the tanks to the river, for Mr. Hathaway was mighty kind to the boys and between heats at the forge told them how he ironed the battleship Morgan, which, armed with six-pounder cannon, went forth to quell Lake Michigan's Mormon rebellion on Beaver Island. Finally, he called the boys together and told them that some of the Mormons in retaliation seemed to be camping on the opposite bank of the river armed with spy glasses, and he would suggest they keep within bounds or he would have to put blinds on the factory.

Perhaps after all, Mr. Hathaway collected dividends on the salt wells in the fun he had with the boys.

Colonel George Lee

Among the first men I became acquainted with after coming to the Rapids was George Lee, a clerk or assistant cashier

THE YESTERDAYS

in Daniel Ball's bank, which occupied a frame building on the present site of the Old National bank. Before and after office hours Mr. Lee came to the shipyard and forge, where at any vacant work-bench he made canoe paddles, fish rods and spear poles. He never interfered with the men and they all liked him.

William Renwick at the same time was trying to make reels and jointed rods for bass casting and they often worked together.

Grand river was the fisherman's paradise. The river bed below the dam was filled with large boulders, between which the waters swirled and any quiet pool behind a rock was sure to be harboring a hungry bass. Men fished from a canoe, one man poling from the stern and another casting from the bow. This required a skill only gained by practice.

Before Mr. Lee married we went out often together in my canoe in the early morning hours. Mother broiled our bass and gave us hot beaten biscuit for breakfast. He was ten years older than I and when he married our pleasure on the river was somewhat interrupted, even before the Civil war called us away.

Mr. Lee helped organize a company for the second regiment of cavalry and as a lieutenant and adjutant began a career in the army of the Cumberland in 1862 under the eyes of Gen. Sheridan.

It was my fortune to serve in Sheridan's division and there again our acquaintance was renewed and nearly two years of my service was in close contact with Adjt. Lee. He was exacting but unfailing in his kindness to the home boys and gave us many opportunities for service and adventure.

Lee was also popular with Sheridan who let no day pass without an invitation to a test of skill with the enemy's outposts. Sheridan was very impetuous and Lee quiet and self-controlled and the brigade and regimental commanders were soon calling Lee the general's balance wheel. As his adjutant he kept the books and the general planned the combats and battles.

Lee advanced in rank and the eagles of a cavalryman rested on his shoulders when the scourge of yellow fever carried him off in 1867 at New Orleans. Lee did not return to Grand Rapids at the close of the war but remained in the regular service as the chief of Gen. Sheridan's staff.

There might not have been a Sheridan so renowned had it not been for the bank clerk, the lieutenant of the Second Michigan cavalry, the surviving members of which are on a trot down the pike and there will soon be no one to write the story of this Michigan boy who rode with Sheridan from the cotton fields of Mississippi to "Winchester town," where they rallied a panic stricken army and headed it back to victory.

More than thirty years ago there came to me in one of the committee rooms at the national capitol a quiet little woman saying, "I am Mary Lee."

What memories the name recalled! Mrs. Lee was serving as a clerk in one of the war department divisions. Her small pension as the widow of this gallant officer was not enough to maintain her. It became my privilege, as a member of the military committee, to make a small return for all the bait George Lee had cast upon the waters, and, with Uncle Sam's assistance Mary Lee was made comfortable for the rest of her life.

Lieutenant Robert Wilson

Because of my warm friendship with Robert Wilson during and after the Civil war I feel a desire to tell something of this man who, as a reporter on the Daily Eagle, tagged "Grab Corners" and made the locality a far-reaching byword.

Chicago's famous Rookery was often sold to hay seeds, but I never heard of a bargain hunter buying Grab Corners after Wilson advertised it in the Eagle.

Artemas Ward with his "wax figures" was not a word better than Bob Wilson and his little stories of the things he saw about Grab Corners, at that time the concentration point of the town's activities.

But just about the time "downtown" was beginning to quake under the honest truth of Bob's busy pen, the war came

THE YESTERDAYS

our way and I touched elbows with him in days when shivers chased up our spinal cords and something besides green persimmons puckered our lips until we couldn't whistle.

I'll tell you of a day when his shock of red hair turned pink. It was during the last days of the war when we were in the tar heel country with Sherman's army. I was in command of a detail from Carlin's division and Lieut. Wilson commanded thirty men from the Twenty-first Michigan.

It had been a day of combats with Dibbrell's Confederate cavalry. These fellows called themselves Dibbrell's cavaliers, gentlemen at the beginning of the war, for each one had a contraband to pick the gray backs off their shirt collars and shine their boots. Near sundown we drove the enemy away from an apple jack still on the Yadkin river. There was a loaded scow of barrels of the jack ready to float down the stream and on to Confederate supply depots. This was why the enemy was so slow in leaving. Apple jack is not sure death but a pint cup of it puts a man out of the fight for twenty hours. The lady of the mill told us the Confederates were fairly sleeping in their saddles as they forded the stream and disappeared over the hill.

My orders for the day were to exterminate the outlaw, Peters, a terror to North Carolina Union men. We were within twenty miles of his home with men and horses exhausted but our only chance to win was by a night ride. Our lady gave me the directions; also, "be careful to shoot first, for Peters is an ornery cuss."

Then came Wilson to say that our boys were so full of apple jack they could not mount, Wilson and the other lieutenants were the only men fit for duty. While they began knocking in the heads of the apple jack barrels Wilson and I mounted on fresh horses and rode away in the night, comforted with the thought that Dibbrell's men also were full of trouble.

We arrived at the outlaw's home after daylight. A woman met us at the door. Inside there was a scurrying of feet not unlike a cross roads schoolhouse at recess. We entered, Colts in hand, prepared to have the first shot. On a bed in the main room was an old grandmother with six frightened children crowded against the wall behind her. No sign of a man. The woman declared her husband had gone to the hills on hearing that Sherman was in the state. But there was a curtain about the lower part of the bed and we both saw it move. Bob dropped on one knee and took aim, while I, with revolver in hand, crept up and yanked the curtain, expecting to face a gun. But there was only another half-dozen wild-eyed children, clad mostly in cotton shirts.

That was a close call for both sides. With three years of army discipline behind us and all sorts of warfare, we wobbled out and ordered the largest boy to bring some drinking water from the spring.

While the woman was baking us a pone we fed our horses at the corncrib and searched the place well for Peters. It was no wonder to us that he was an outlaw, for it was the most forsaken spot in the world. For miles on the return Wilson said not a word except "Captain, wish I had a canteen of that apple jack."

Not long after this ride, Wilson, leading his command in a desperate charge, stopped a musket ball that sent him home to Michigan, where he lived only a few years, never fully recovering from his wounds.

In 1866 he was elected city clerk, but Mayor Wilder D. Foster still hailed him as Bob, as did nearly everybody, for they loved him, but those of us who slept in the leaves under the trees, drinking from the same canteen with him, knew him best.

His bits of poetry, stories, sarcasm and wit, like a bubbling spring from a mountain side, ended only when he found the trail's end.

Colonel Christofer W. Leffingwell and His Troop of Cavalry

Col. Leffingwell was a United States cavalryman with a record of active service in the Mexican war. He had the gaunt, sinewy frame that one sees portrayed by Frederick Remington in his types of plainsman soldier and he was a fine horseman. In the late fifties he organized a troop of cavalry that was the admiration of all the young people of the town.

There was abundant material available, plenty of willing men and many fine saddle horses. Also a good drill ground on the creek bottom lands on the west side of the river, south of Bridge-st. A creek ran along two sides and a slight plateau on the south made a fine reviewing stand for the public.

In the annals of the state, so far as I know, there is no roster of Leffingwell's troop. There were three active companies of infantry and one of artillery recognized by the state, but there were two war clouds in the air—the rumblings from the Mormons in Utah and the black cloud south of Mason and Dixon's line—and every man who had had experience in the army knew that the horse must play an important part in either conflict. Although assured that the state could not equip or recognize a cavalry troop at the time, the colonel's first call brought out thirty well mounted men. One drill brought ten files of fours into line.

The colonel had sons enough of his own to make another file, but lacked the mounts. The town was just of a size for every person to know every other person, so we knew by name every man as they formed on the north side of the field, counted fours and advanced company front toward the creek.

The colonel gave his commands in a voice that could have controlled a full battalion. They were a peppery lot, too, on fine Morgan horses and were soon working from the walk to a trot, then fours left and gallop into line.

The town took a great interest in the troop and all the ladies were on hand for drill, applauding and encouraging their heroes.

One fine afternoon the command "fours left" failed to be given, but the men were game, into the creek they went, some taking headers, others keeping their saddles but floundering in the mire. Only a man who has been in just such a fix can appreciate what took place before the troop could again be lined up before its commander. Then with the colonel in the lead they filed into the nearby river, dismounted and washed the mud from themselves and their much loved animals.

That evening the troop held a symposium. As I was only a young boy I was not admitted and to this day do not know whether this charge was a blunder or a matter of discipline, but since all the minor officers went into the creek with the troop I imagine it was a blunder.

The people of the city did not realize that these men were training to become leaders in the greatest cavalry battle the world has ever known. Nearly every man of the troop served either with Sheridan or Custer and they won rank from lieutenant to general. Many of them went down on fields where the sabers clashed.

Col. Leffingwell returned to the regular service for the entire Civil war. His son, Henry, and I were comrades on the grand review in Washington at the close of the struggle. Some of the men of this troop that I recall are Miles Adams, George Gray, C. P. Babcock, Herb Backus, Stephen Ballard, Guild and Robert Barr, Charles Bolza, Byron Brewer, C. W. Calkins, C. W. Eaton, John Ely, H. W. Granger, Birney Hoyt, George Lee, Dan Littlefield, I. C. Smith, Silas Pierce, Peter Weber and Don Lovell. If their tales of the war could be told there would be pages of romance, loyalty to country, stories of days when chivalry was in the saddle and Americans were crossing swords with Americans.

Of all that troop I recall but one man who seemed to have any creek bottom mud clinging to him. At home he had two fine saddle horses, but on foot he could run faster and further, to get away from the firing line, than any other man in the regiment in which it was my good fortune to serve.

The old drill ground is now covered with factories. The creek has been lost in the "big ditch" and the ditch swallowed by the sewer, but the flag of the nation floats from the top of the staff.

The Annals of Fulton Street Park

I have before me as I write an old-time print of Samuel Dexter, who in 1832 came to Michigan from Herkimer, N. Y., as the leader of a party looking for lands where its members might settle and make homes.

THE YESTERDAYS

Mr. Dexter journeyed beyond the Rapids, following the river and the shore of Lake Michigan as far as Chicago and then returning with his party located government land at the Rapids and Ionia.

The following year he conducted sixty-one others, many of whom found Ionia the more attractive locality.

Mr. Dexter's face is of a character that inspires one to follow his leadership, eyes that smile and the straightforward look in which one places confidence.

Many of his descendants living in Grand Rapids and in Ionia county bear the same interesting features and have from the first days of the settlement of the valley been prominent in the development of Western Michigan.

These people did not come as traders, but to create homes in the wilderness and build up the grand country we now love so well. They came as workers of the soil and their descendants are proud to say they came with Samuel Dexter. The wealth of the forests, on the other hand, was responsible for the speculators who flocked to Michigan for investments in pine timber lands.

Mr. Dexter bought from the government a strip of land eighty rods wide and two miles long running north and west from the present corner of Monroe-av. and Division-av. The deeds of record were signed by President Andrew Jackson.

The same year he met a commission appointed by the governor of Michigan to locate a county seat for Kent. The state commission selected, and Mr. Dexter and his wife, Anna, gave to the County of Kent the parcel of land which for many years has been called Fulton-st. park. At that time Monroe and Fulton-sts. were Indian trails.

At one of the court trials years after, brought in an effort to annul the county's title, Zenas Windsor testified he saw Samuel Dexter drive the stake in the center of the square chosen. All the vicinity then was a forest of elm, oak and hickory, which in the eyes of land speculators had small commercial value but presented a level, well drained plateau.

In this square, in the year 1838, the first courthouse was built, costing about $3,000. It is described as of Greek temple design, tall columns at the front, facing south, a cupola with a gilded ball on the top and bell inside, a hall through the center with a stairway at the east end leading to the courtroom above. On the first floor were the sheriff's living rooms and a jail room of planks and sheet iron ribbing. This building with all its records was burned in 1844.

Then the county, being hard up, built a sort of cross roads schoolhouse, so small that the rapidly accumulating records were stored in any vacant room about the town until 1850.

The county held undisputed use of the square and rented this building for any public gathering. One year it earned fifty dollars. The supervisors sold the foundation stones of the first building and until 1881 were at sea, very sick most of the time, casting up resolutions and committees and always too poor or timid to hazard an investment in a county courthouse. During this period the county "peddled fish," short changed the treasury by paying rent for a west side jail site and express charges on clothes baskets and flour barrels full of official records, some of which for convenience were stored in basement saloons.

All thoughts of ever using the square for a county building were abandoned.

Annals of Fulton Street Park—II

The Samuel Dexter plat as part of the city contains much besides boundaries. Its courthouse square, Fulton park, although but a block in the heart of the city, is rich in the lore of the county. Its history is a tale of entanglements well told in the official city, county and court records which disclose men sparring for financial and political advantage with a vim that would make interesting copy for the sport page of a Sunday edition.

In the suits that were brought by different parties for possession of courthouse square after it had become valuable property, it was testified that Ezekiel Davis, supervisor for Grand Rapids, and Julius C. Abel, supervisor for Grandville, contracted to build the first courthouse for $3,000.

But as typical of the early days the testimony of Robert

Hilton, one of the solid men of the town, is very interesting. It seems the county was hard up for cash and after much effort succeeded in borrowing $4,500 from the state. Mr. Hilton, who owned a single wagon and horse, was sent to Detroit for the money that the building might be erected. The roads were poor, the days wet and sultry and Mr. Hilton was nearly a week returning with the money which on arrival, was found to be mildewed. Moreover it was "wildcat" times and during the week the bank which issued the cat skins had failed. It was probable the printer could not keep up with the disbursing clerk.

The county tried many years to have this debt canceled and more than doubled the original debt in attorney fees and traveling expenses before the cats ceased squalling, then submitted to the loss.

There were many courthouse projects that did not favor this site, but the square was used for almost everything, including several county fairs, and one summer the city officials permitted a circus to set tents for a two days' show. The circus ring was where the first courthouse had stood. Tradition reports complimentary tickets to the city officials and five dollars to the treasury.

The circus departed in the night and the nearby neighbors were a year in cleaning up the refuse. They dug up the hatchet for the aldermen of the west side and north ends of the city, who, to quiet them, passed an ordinance forbidding cattle and swine running at large in the public square. The animals evidently were not notified, for the ordinance was not observed. That however, was the last circus to dig a ring in the square. A short time after another council voted one hundred dollars to improve the park on condition that private subscription should fence it.

It might have been a bit of sarcasm on the part of the county supervisors aimed at the want of business sense displayed by the city supervisors which caused them to petition the state legislature to locate the county seat at Plainfield, then a lumber town near the mouth of the River Rouge. They sent a log rolling committee to the legislature and had not

Grand Rapids taken notice Plainfield would have been placed on the map.

They did not get the county seat, but years later, did get Bert McAuley's clubhouse, which was much better than any county building for good cheer and chicken dinners.

About this time one or two county fairs were held on the square. Bulls with nose rings were chained to the trees, blue ribbon swine rooted for acorns, golden pumpkins were displayed under the oaks and country and city boys vied with one another in gingerbread devotion to the prettiest girl.

Annals of Fulton Street Park—III

My personal touch with the courthouse square began in 1854 when as a boy I rambled across lots on the way to school on Fountain-st. In the center of the square were the foundation stones of the first courthouse, which had burned.

Boys pointed to the place close by where a scaffold had been erected upon which a man was to be executed for killing an Indian, and we discussed the need of a scaffold when there were so many good oaks with low branches.

The story was told that Thomas Gilbert, the sheriff, did not believe the man guilty and used his best efforts to have the law of capital punishment changed. He was slow in having the scaffold finished. The execution was to be a public affair and many people came in from the country only to be disappointed, for the governor commuted the sentence to life imprisonment. Later, Mr. Gilbert found evidence to prove the man was innocent and he was pardoned.

In Civil war days, rough stands were erected in the square where war talks and songs inspired the boys and men. On these rude platforms Mrs. Lavancha Stone Shedd, Mrs. Serepta Bliss Wenham, Miss Jan Ringuette Malloch and many other well known women led the singing.

There were bonfires, about which gathered the boys and girls whose fathers were marching away to battle for the Union. That indeed was the place where the people rallied around the flag.

In the centennial year a fac-simile of the La Framboise

cabin, which in 1806 was standing near the Council Pine on the west bank of the river, was built on the southeast corner of the square. It was carried out in detail even to the coon and fox skins tacked on the outside, but the cabin was neglected and served mainly as a place for the boys to re-enact war dances and shoot arrows at neighbors' pigs and chickens.

For many years the square received no attention other than being a battle-ground for the city and county officials. Citizens petitioned for permission to fence and clean it up, build walks and plant trees. Through the determination of Thomas D. Gilbert to save the park the authorities gave him the care of it for two years. To him we owe the maples as well as those which were about Monument park. At his own expense he hired John Steketee with his yoke of oxen to plow the square for two seasons, paying eight dollars each year and taking great care that the trees were not injured. To subdue the weeds and level the surface he planted potatoes one year and sowed oats another, later plowing the oats under for fertilizer.

After Mr. Gilbert had it in good shape the council ordered the marshal to repair the fence and then to put locks on the gates. Young ladies with their beaus who wished to walk through the park climbed the fence—no small adventure in hoop skirt days.

Mr. Gilbert was an officer and stockholder of the gas company and about this time the council ordered the gas-meter removed and substituted kerosene lamps for summer evenings.

As Mr. Gilbert could get no park seats, he paid the marshal for capping the fence with strips which made a sort of roosting place for young people and soon the fence was worn out. In the year 1881 for some reason the county supervisors replaced the fence and five days later the city marshal tore it up, leaving the post holes for night walkers to fall into. Then Mr. Gilbert hired and paid a man to keep cattle and swine from again destroying the grass and trees. With his own hands he set out young trees, carrying water in pails to moisten their roots. They were his children and were protected and nourished with every care. He had a vision of the future, the day that is here now.

OF GRAND RAPIDS

Annals of Fulton Street Park—IV

In the early platting of the city, Monroe-st., now avenue, was named as a compliment to President James Monroe, whose home on Prince-st., New York City, is now marked with a bronze table but occupied as an Italian rag picker's warehouse. Jefferson-av. was named in honor of Thomas Jefferson, Fulton-st. as a compliment to Robert Fulton, the inventor of steamboats, also a resident of New York. He never, so far as we know, placed his feet on Michigan soil.

There was an early settler in the town named Fulton, but since he came here after the first plats were made and was noted only for the gingerbread he baked at a shop in the bend of lower Monroe-av., it is not likely that he had any claim on Fulton-st.

The slogan, "Grand Rapids is a Good Place to Live," is a fact. The city has been made a good place through the influence and generosity of its public spirited men and women, some of whom we have honored.

We have the John Ball, the Garfield, Comstock, Campau, Harrison, Sinclair and Wilcox parks; the Robinson road, the Burton Heights, the Hodenpyl woods, the Richmond hills, the Mary Waters field, the Blodgett and Butterworth hospitals, the Stocking and Widdicomb schools and many other places are or should be bearing the names of those who have made Grand Rapids a good place to live.

It is not too late to change the name of Fulton-st. park to that of Samuel Dexter and thus honor the almost first settler who gave that square of ground to the County of Kent for the benefit of all its people. Mr. Fulton could still have his street —a very creditable possession.

A simple authoritative resolution of the city commission, one that would call for no appropriation of public money, would be the means of preserving this name.

We have cause for rejoicing that in 1896, the bronze bust of Thomas D. Gilbert, a gift of the National City Bank and the Grand Rapids Gas Co., two local business enterprises which he was instrumental in establishing, was placed in the park beneath the maples which he had planted and so lovingly cared for.

Hundreds of boys, young and old, listened to President James B. Angell's story of the man, from the time he captained a pole boat on Grand river with Indians for a crew, to the day when the bronze bust was placed in the park.

I am indebted to Miss Belle M. Tower's true history of Fulton-st. park, contributed to Sophie De Marsac chapter, Daughters of the American Revolution, 1910, for many of the facts recorded in these annals to which I have added my personal memories. Miss Tower is a granddaughter of Samuel Dexter.

The Elm Trees

An article in one of our daily papers of recent date states that no less an authority than Michaux—a tree lover of national fame—ranks the common white elm of our country as one of its most magnificent trees. From coast to coast, from Canada's border to the gulf, it is unsurpassed, whether in forest, open field or at the roadside. In New England parkways and college grounds they have sacred memories and are guarded with all the care that man can give.

In days gone by there were some wonderful groves of white elm on the west side of Grand river, extending along the river from Sixth street to Mill Creek and one grove south of Fulton street with both dome and umbrella tops. All about the valley were groups, or single fine specimens, with the turban and plume tops.

I recall the groves in the glory of their autumn yellow, when their light rivaled the sun in the Indian summer haze.

In the early days of the country, the elm was often the range guide to homesteader, surveyors, or the Indian. Before the pier and range lights marked the channel to Black lake a single huge elm guided the sailor. The Indian by the bending of a branch often indicated a direction and many of the strange shaped limbs of the river bottom trees were the work of surveyors or early trail markers and have served for years to indicate the boundary of a range. As the twig was bent so the tree grew.

Standing like a lone sentinel on the range of the Cascade Hills Golf Club is a grand fountain-topped white elm and we trust it will be an honorary member of long standing in that organization.

More than fifty years ago when Bostwick street hill was being graded there were in the roadway in front of the homes of James and Ezra Nelson, two very fine elm trees. Their branches entwining made wonderful shade for the street and a place for swings which the firemen of the hook and ladder company suspended for the boys and girls of the vicinity.

When this grading was started the city council in a fit of mental aberration directed the "highway man" to remove the trees from the roadway. A storm of protest came from all sides, but seemed to have little effect on the council and when it came to a showdown between the highway men or trees, the Nelsons, who were full sized men, loaded their guns with rock salt and unground black pepper and stood guard day and night.

Mr. E. D. G. Holden also came to the rescue with a poem which was printed and scattered far and wide. His listening ear caught the murmuring of the brother elms and this is a part of what they said:

"Why, yes, dear chum, I mind it well
With red men camping here
Beneath our shade when time had made
Our forms a landmark dear.
We saw the scalp dance and the love
Of Indian maids for braves
Who made no threats to slash us down.
Oh, it will be a sorry day
If they should cut us down,
Who are the oldest settlers now
In all the busy town.
We never yet an ill have done,
The good we love the best,
And pleased are we when children pause
Upon the walk to rest
With welcome shade caressed."

THE YESTERDAYS

So the ax was exchanged for shovels, the ground about the trees was rounded up, the roadway graded on either side and today we still have the Bostwick, often termed by the old residents the Nelson, elms gracing the city highway.

The Blendon Hills

About eighteen miles below the Rapids, on the south side of the river, are the Blendon Hills, in the early days noted for their forests of oaks and pine.

The lumbermen went through the pines on some tracts, selecting only the best of the trees and from these only the clear stock, making a jungle with the cuttings on the ground and leaving a maze of tote roads and blind trails. As if by magic these cut-over lands were quickly covered with a growth of high-bush blackberry brush, loaded every season with delicious fruit.

Many townspeople went berrying, paddling by canoe or going down the river in the steamboats. Sometimes parties formed with an outfit for camping out, and over the campfire put up tubs and jars of blackberry jam; others stayed over night and returned home to preserve the fruit.

One day eight or ten of us twelve-year-old boys paddled away from the yellow warehouse with a two or three-day outfit—one tent, blankets and baskets of rations, a butcher knife or two to kill bears or maybe Indians—the bravest bunch of boys that ever said goodbye to the mothers who had helped carry the duffle to the dock.

It was afternoon when the fleet landed at Blendon and to carry everything up the river bank, set up the tent and get the first meal was a great event. Some of the boys ate up half of their two days' rations that first meal. They were busy cutting hemlock for beds and gathering wood for a campfire until nearly dark, when an Indian we knew about town landed in his canoe and while he cooked a fish over our fire for his supper, told the crowd a bear story—a real thriller. He assured us that bears lived on blackberries and that all the pine slashings were full of them. While he talked he sandwiched in a loaf of our bread with his fish. When he left, Eddie Morrison and Henry

Leffingwell fixed up the fire. We got inside, tied down the flaps and tested our knives.

Billie Westerhouse was used to sleeping between feather ticks and the hemlock boughs didn't appeal to him, but he finally got settled under the blankets just as all the owls between Haire's Landing and Lamont began to hoot and call. One little kid began to cry for his mother, but the finishing touch to the crowd was the falling of a rotten basswood tree a few rods from the tent. Just why it came down on that night of all others is not to be explained, but sun-up found us on the way home with a fine load of stories of the bears and Indians who had tried to sever our earthly connections, but never a blackberry for the mothers.

The Fitch family, living at the corner of Stocking and Bridge-sts., were berrying in Blendon Hills, when Cordelia —as I recall, about a sixteen-year-old girl—became lost in the slashings. The alarm went out and for three days all the campers were searching. The steamboat reported at the Rapids and every available skiff came loaded with helpers, among them several Indians.

I hunted with one of the Indian boys and we got caught several miles from camp as night came on. He crawled under a small cedar and fastened all the boughs together and we slept as comfortably as in a tent. The third day Cordelia was seen by a steamboat crew on the river bank fourteen miles below Blendon, though "wild like deer," as one Indian explained.

She disappeared again in the forest and it was only after a race that she was captured, her clothing torn to rags on the brambles and briers. She lived to become the bride of Edward L. Briggs and to furnish our Kent Scientific Museum with a fine collection of shells and rare treasures from many lands.

The Blendon Pines and Oaks

In the early days of the settlement of the Grand river country, eastern capitalists were told of the wealth of Michigan forests, to be obtained for a song.

The pine was what the speculator sought and many personally or through agents bought up vast tracts.

THE YESTERDAYS

John Ball had little money of his own but was the trusted agent for many. He was a born woodsman and the happiest days of his long and useful life were spent in companionship of the trees.

In one of his early adventures, he sought a forest of pine reported to be south of the Grand river, between the Rapids and Lake Michigan, which only Indians and trappers had invaded; a region of rivers, lakes, swamps and level plateaus where the tree tops were so dense that the sun rarely penetrated. The surveys were largely guesswork. In 1836 Mr. Ball sought this tract but found a wonderful forest of oak and in a three days' tramp only an occasional lonesome pine. This oak covered the hills known later as Blendon, eighteen miles down Grand river. Then suddenly the pines were before him.

Mr. Ball at once entered at the land office, probably the one at Ionia, a claim to forty-one eighty-acre lots, paying the entry fee and other requirements. He reached, however, the limits of his capital and was finally compelled to forfeit his payments and other parties secured the lands.

Several years later Robert Medler, ship builder, needed oak for the yard at Mill Point, near the Haven. Men went into this oak forest and helped themselves. Standing trees had so little value that no one objected. In fact, there was only the government to object and its agents were far away. The logs on the high banks of the river when rolled into the water sank like so much iron. To float them a pine was pinned to either side and they were floated to the shipyards. There the builders claimed them to be live oak and Capt. Flint, U. S. naval contractor, accepted them as such in the construction of the U. S. bark Morgan.

I do not know the origin of the name Blendon but the Blendon Lumber Co. was formed and a rush made to secure the oaks. Logging camps, sawmills, landing docks and shipyards sprang up and the entire country boomed. Pioneer farmers found a ready market for everything they raised.

Two-masted lumber schooners towed up the river by tugs received the lumber direct from the mill, towed back to the lake and sailed away to the sea. Often rafts of long masts were towed which eventually fitted ocean ships.

The men who came out of the east to lumber this new country were equal to the trees they made war upon.

When the Civil war called, Alvin C. Litchfield, manager of the Blendon company, captained one of the companies and under Custer won the star of a general. Out of this country went the Brennans, Weatherwaxes, Lowings, Boyntons and so many others that there were none left on the farms or in the mills. The quietude of Sunday settled over the land.

After war days, the echoes of the ax and saw, the chanty of the river man and the farmer were heard again until the last oak and pine disappeared. In their stead came the cabin, the apple tree, and the honey bee. And finally came the man in the speed wagon, all unconscious of the past were it not for the stump fences which say so little but mean so much to the few who understand.

Mr. Foster, one of the six-foot lumbermen who served with the Old Third infantry, is living in the city today. He can take you to a pine stump six feet across the top, the living tree of which was more than one hundred feet to the first limb.

The Walnut Forest

There were three classes of men who came from the east to Michigan in the early days. The settler who came to make a home—he was the man who came to stay, the foundation of the state; the trader who sought a fortune in the wild life of the forest, the furs of the beaver and his kin; the speculator who recognized the value of the great wilderness of pine forest.

It seemed as if all the wealth in eastern money centers was brought here to be invested in the pine.

River bottom lands were thickly grown with walnut, butternut and great elms; ridges were covered with oak and cherry, and the plateaus with maple and all sorts of valuable trees, but the speculator saw little value in them as compared with the pine. The hemlock was a poor relation and treated with small courtesy.

As late as the fifties, the present site of the Wyoming car

shops was a forest of butternut trees growing so thickly that often it was fifty feet to the first limb. After a sharp frost the ground was brown with nuts, on the opposite side of the river were forests of giant walnut.

A settler in order to clear a place to grow corn slashed these walnut in tangled masses, felling them across each other and, using the old term "niggered," burned them into sections. They were too large to saw into lengths.

Great clear logs were split into fence rails; others were hewed into barns sills. In the tree tops were huge limb crotches which had a value if sliced into veneers. Men came and hewed some of these free from sap and bark. With oxen they were taken to the river, loaded on scows and floated to the Haven, then by other ways transported to Boston, where furniture men worked them up. Most of the clear body of these trees were burned in the fields to get rid of them.

There were several gunsmiths then in the Rapids. Soloman Pierce and his sons had cords of fine walnut burl gun stocks and seasoned them in the yard outside to acquire the amber color so sought for by sportsmen.

But the walnut was never so grand as when it stood in the green woodland, its wide spreading top far in the sky, its almost black bark coating dark against the background of an oak grown hillside.

Wise men of those days warned against the destruction of the forests, but the near-sighted believed Michigan could never clear away the wilderness.

The Indian looked upon the waste as a crime. He inherited a reverence for all trees, assigned to them passions and believed in a close connection between human lives and trees. When the wigwam was built a branch from a nearby tree was placed at the doorway so the spirit of the forest would be with its inmates.

In money value Michigan lost more in fifty years than can ever be regained and if it was in the plans of the Man-i-to that the great lakes country should make the furniture of the world the early settler and the lumberjack certainly played a chuck-a-luck game with the treasury.

OF GRAND RAPIDS

The Black Hills

In the south part of the city is a range of hills, with the river front on the west, Plaster creek, Wyoming yards and their great shops on the south, the Pere Marquette tracks running around the base of the hill on the east, the Peaceful valley with its many factories, the Michigan railway bridge and the great hive of industry toward the city on the north.

When I was a boy this river range hill was the home of the Ottawa Indian chief, Mack-e-bee-messy, which translated is Black Bird. So this hill was to the Indian "Black Bird's Hill." Its wide plateau was covered with a forest of black oak and the white man coming in called the range Black Oak hills. From these terms it simply settled into plain Black hills, and so it is known today.

The Indians had a way of burning the leaves late each autumn, as they lay over the ground, the flames taking the lower branches of the trees and all the summer growth. When the spring rains began the new season the forest was a sylvan glory. On level ground one could see any moving thing a mile away.

The river bottom and all low lying places were thickly grown with elm, basswood and water maple, with dogwood, thorn and crabapple. The side hill facing the river and much of the plateau was strewn with great water-washed granite boulders, that on the northwest end, spread into the stream forming "Stony Point," which challenged the canoe man to combat with eddies and swirls.

Chief Black Bird, when the treaty was made with the Indians for the Grand River valley, lived in the summer in his wigwam on the northwest point of the hill, far above the river. In the winter he retired to the shelter of a thick grove of spruce standing about where the Nichols & Cox mills are now located.

After the treaty, the white man fenced in the hills with black walnut rails. The granite boulders were split into building stone. Townspeople, attracted by the beautiful woods, came to picnic and gather wild flowers or honey from the store of wild bees.

THE YESTERDAYS

While gathering mushrooms in the north woods not long ago, an old-time resident of the valley said she could tell me of the most wonderful place in all the world for mushrooms and then explained how to reach Black hills. I could not convince her that the city had covered the old playground.

The oaks had no commercial value and as pasture the land did not pay taxes, so the man who had bought the hills from the government, seeing the people congregating there every pleasant day, offered it to the city for park purposes at farm-land price. Our city fathers derided the owner for trying to unload undesirable land on the people. Months of argument failed to convince the aldermen that other years were on the road to town.

Later Mr. Delos A. Blodgett, unable to stand for the destruction of trees, flowers and rocks, determined the city should have the hills as his gift. The price, one hundred thousand dollars, three times what the city previously was asked to pay, was agreed upon with the agent, but the owner, sore over the action of past officials or, as others claimed, profiteering, demanded fifty thousand more. The demand was so unjust that it was emphatically rejected.

Then came years when the hills gave shelter to tramps and hoboes and the undesirables of the country and it was not safe for flower and forest lovers.

This was forty years ago. Today the east plateau of the range is well covered with homes; the west has still a growth of black oak, but the boulders are in foundation stones all over town. The smoke of factory stacks drifts over the bluffs and the haze of Black Bird's wigwam fire is only a memory.

The River Rouge

Fur traders, trappers and French-Canadians with the spirit of adventure, early explored the valley of the O-wash-ta-nong, following the river and its tributaries.

Many of these men descended to the level of the Indian in the habits of wild life, but retained the dialects and memory of home places, which cropped out in the designation of towns and rivers. Many married squaws who were their mates for life, shared in their toil and travel.

Thus the French in River Rouge or River Red, coming into the O-wash-ta-nong—the Grand—near Plainfield, may have been inspired by the wilderness of painted foliage where each tree and flower gave different tinting to the hills and river bottom lands.

Indian traditions told of the white men who came each season with canoes loaded with furs from this stream of many beaver ponds.

These trappers told at the Rapids of the wilderness of great trees of the pine and oak, of the many lakes between the hills where the wild goose nested. From its source in the rice swamps the river ran a wild race between the hills to its blending with the Grand.

When the rush of the lumberman started toward this stream it was not unlike that of the gold seekers of 1849 to the golden west. River bank trees were chopped into the stream and, beaver like, formed sawmill dams and ponds. Rude settlements and lumber towns sprang up over night.

Near the river mouth, under a wonderful bluff overlooking the Grand and facing the morning sun, the Indians had a burial ground where the great spirit could find the dead and guide them on the home road.

Here upon the high plateau the "Mon-daw-min"—Indian corn—was planted, an ear being placed in the grave at the burial time for food on the long journey.

Plainfield seemed the most appropriate name for the town that sprang up here—and so it is today—but for a long time it was called by men in sarcastic mood, Grogtown. To obliterate this term it was given the name Austerlitz for a while.

Following the Rouge up-stream one encountered the mill town of Gibraltar and then Jericho. At both places there was grand water power. As fast as the pines were cut away the land was cleared and platted and our leading statesmen honored in naming of the streets. There were several other mill towns before Laphamville—named from an early settler—was reached, a village of blessed memory, so beautiful in its peace-

THE YESTERDAYS

ful valley. Before the days of highway bridges people crossed the stream at the Rocky ford. Then in later years the name was changed to Rockford. Although it was a mill town it became a home place. The forest disappeared but the charm of the river and the hills held captive many of the pioneers.

Following the winding river it was a long paddle to the home of that good man, Dr. Sexton, who was an angel of mercy to all the inhabitants of cabins and mill shacks of northern Kent. A "God bless you" often paid the bill. It was all the pioneer could offer.

At the last mill site on the river sprang up the town of Gougeburg. It never had or needed any other name. Besides its logging crews there were two lawyers, said by the lumberjacks to be hiding from the sheriff. When not tipping the jug they wove shingles and in public spirited way helped the town live up to its name.

If a man succeeded in escaping from Gougeburg he reached beyond to the Meyers settlement, lying between the river and Camp lake; Hiram, Tom, Ben and Andrew, four brothers, three of them with large families, had come to stay and were making farms. It was often said that no man ever went away from Hiram Meyers' homestead hungry and that Auntie Nicholas Emmons in their cabin on Camp lake served the most delicious fritters and maple syrup that man or boy ever tasted.

At the far end of Camp lake was Snow's tavern. From here crows flying north carried haversacks with frogs for rations, for it was the jumping off place until the trail reached the Muskegon river.

During the forties and the fifties this River Rouge country was a lumberman's battlefield. Harry Ives, a Grand Rapids millwright, with gangs of men packed their tools and supplies from one mill site to another.

Only a fraction of the logs were sawed in the mills. In one season Job Whipple, a captain of the river men and now living in Grandville, floated 165,000,000 feet of logs out of the river to the mills at the Haven. Many of these logs were so large they were three years reaching their destination, hung up on shoals and driftwood jams, their water bleached sides like ghosts haunting the streams.

Only good grade logs were put into the streams, all other were left for forest fires. From one forty-acre lot near Rockford one million feet of logs were cut that scaled two and one-half logs to the thousand feet. When the battle with the forest was over the mill towns vanished and the river men and woodsmen began hoeing corn in fields fenced with stumps.

I never climb one of these fences without looking for a cant-hook or peavie, but find only bittersweet.

Prospect Hill

Prospect hill of pioneer days was a ridge of clay and gravel, evidently of glacial formation, running from Monroe-st. north beyond Lyon. Its height was about seventy feet above the river bed, it was beautifully wooded and made a striking feature in the landscape. It was all leveled in the grading of the city and the Peninsular club, the Michigan Trust building and the City Hall are in line with and stand on what was formerly the base of the hill.

Along in the fifties Prospect hill was the playground of the uptown boys, even into city days, the Lyon and Pearl-sts. slopes were favorite coasting places for boys and girls.

There were several ponds about its base, the best one fed by springs was on the east side of the hill. Here Gay Perkins, Charlie Leonard and Dan Tower skated in winter and manned pirate crafts in summer, using garden gates for raft foundation and fence pickets for propellers.

One of the first men to build a home on the hill was George Martin, or as he was known later, Judge Martin. He had a large, fine frame house on the crest of the hill with porches on three sides. From the porch on the west side we could look through the trees and in the evening watch the wigwam fires on the islands and the jack lights of the fishermen spearing in the river rapids.

The Martins had three boys, Billie, George and Charlie, and one girl, May, and they were very cordial to visitors.

The house was usually overflowing with guests. The boys

made their own sleds at the shipyard forge, using scrap lumber from Deacon Haldane's cabinet shop. If I remember correctly they made the first pair of bobs used on the hill, walnut runners and a black cherry board, probably thrown into the culls because there was a knot or two in it.

There was considerable trouble over the timber on the hill and the strife over the honey salvaged from several bee trees reached as far as the justice courts. Charlie Martin fell from a tree where he was trying to capture a coon and broke his leg. There was a near lawsuit over the girdling of some black cherry trees, the fact that their bark soaked in a whisky keg made a tonic for warding off ague being no excuse for the vandalism.

There were many beautiful specimens of oak, hickory and basswood trees on the hill and about the base on all sides many great elms and butternuts.

Among the guests at the Martin house, was Daniel Thompson, a writer of novels. He was a lawyer, but did not work at the trade. While visiting on Prospect hill he wrote "May Martin," in compliment to the little daughter of the house; "The Green Mountain Boys," "The Gold Diggers" and several other stories for boys and girls. Prospect hill featured in many of his tales of the wilderness. He seemed to find the village full of interesting people and made many friends.

Though the ridge gradually was leveled, it was 1890 before the last of it was carted away. The banging of a shotgun through that district today would cause more consternation to the street loiterer than it ever did to the squirrels and rabbits of that happy forest of childhood days.

Professor Edward W. Chesebro

There is in Oak Hill cemetery a monument erected to the memory of Prof. Edward W. Chesebro by his pupils, bearing this inscription:

> "His was a teacher's heart
> With zeal that never tired,
> And thousand souls beat higher
> By his single soul inspired."

The first school I attended on coming to Grand Rapids was on Fountain-st. hill, the High school of the town. It had three study and six recitation rooms. There was no basement to the building. It was heated by wood stoves. Drinking water was brought from a side hill spring in a pail and all the pupils drank from the same dipper.

Mr. Chesebro was the principal and with rare good judgment selected the teachers who assisted him. The years in which he served were a trying time in the history of the schools. The town was growing rapidly, but no funds could be gained to build and equip buildings. The small salary of teachers was often paid by school orders, passed at the stores at a discount or in payment for merchandise at a high profit.

The country school teacher who boarded around the district as part pay for service, had an advantage over the city teacher. The farmer as a general rule had plenty of food.

The crowded school rooms, poorly ventilated, and heated by wood stoves, with board floors where scores of muddy boots left a trail of soil, were not a pleasant atmosphere in which to work. The entire burden of school management fell on Mr. Chesebro's shoulders. Men and women of today could hardly be found to do the tasks imposed upon the principal and his assistants.

He literally wore himself out in establishing the foundation that others have built upon and was laid away in 1862, not surviving the pioneering days.

The old playgrounds and my old playmates, come clearly to my mind. There was only an acre of sand lot on the sand hill bluffs for play grounds and half this space was piled high with wood for the stoves. The girls managed to get in a few swings but most of the place looked like a prairie dog village, where various clans of boys dug in tunnels and made fortifications for their battles.

This congestion led to some of the boys going outside the fence to the bluffs, even as far from school as the present site of Crescent-pk. Here in a bunch of oak grubs, Richard Blumrich, Henry Leffingwell, and Henry Rounds tunneled through a point in the hill and felt they had a safe retreat from any hostile clan. There one noon Henry Rounds, who was mostly legs, was caught by a cave-in and only his feet left in sight. His mates began frantically pulling at the legs. A Dutchman who owned the lot, advised them to wait while he ran to the brewery for a shovel, but the boys with bare hands, succeeded in digging him out and by the time the shovel was at hand every known way of getting sand out of a cave man and air into him, was being applied.

The boys were an hour late and when they gave their reason Prof. Chesebro called all the boys of the class to the study room and gave them a life saving talk. He did not approve of caves on the bluffs but he commended the bravery of the boys who had stood by their playmate. From that time on he made a stand for better playgrounds.

Grand Rapids could well afford the tribute of a Chesebro avenue leading to a modern school and playground.

The Stone Schoolhouse

Along in the fifties it became necessary to enlarge the schoolhouse on the west side of the river, so the wise men of the school board decided to build large enough for all time. River stone was plenty and cost only the digging and hauling; building lumber was a drug on the market and good mechanics one dollar per day of ten hours.

The school was built where the Union High now is. The top, or third floor, was used for the Armory; each lower floor had a large study room and two recitation rooms. In the large rooms were two box stoves—one on the girls' and one on the boys' side of the room—which burned two-foot wood usually carried upstairs by the boys. The tuition of the country boys was often paid with wood.

The stoves were in one corner of the room and the pipe ran to the other corner overhead, so no heat was lost. When the men drilled in the Armory above, the vibrations parted the pipe joints and the soot sifted down upon the pupils of Prof. Boardman Taylor's night school; special classes for spelling and penmanship were very popular because it gave the boys a chance to beau the girls home.

There was no janitor at first and when one was supplied, he was known as the moderator and assisted the principal when he got hold of a boy he could not manage single handed.

Everything was lovely in the spring and fall, when the older boys worked outside, but in the winter when they came in from the country the principal went armed with a six-foot hickory pointer. The moderator earned his salary, for in the battles the stove and all its pipe frequently came down. The small boys crawled under the desks and the older ones tried to be neutral. They wanted to see the country chaps downed but could not forget that the same hickory pointer often beat the dust out of their own trousers. Some of the principals were short term men, the length of service depending upon their muscle. Prof. Ballard, Prof. Clark, and Prof. Kent stayed the longest, but they really applied tact along with zeal and stick.

The schoolyard, inclosed by a board fence with a post entrance at either corner—not so much to keep the pupils in as to keep the cows and pigs out—was one city block in size except for the home of Mrs. Stephen Cool, who owned two lots at the corner of Turner and Fourth. She had declined to give these up but the board was not much concerned since the nearest well and supply of water was on her ground. She had a fine vegetable garden and was a lover of flowers and chickens. As the school grew her corner became quite a problem. She was at war with the boys all the time. They batted their balls through the windows, trampled the garden down and that sweet two hundred-pound woman was worried to a frazzle but could not be persuaded to sell out and go to a quieter locality.

All the school ground west of the building was piled high with cord wood for the winter fire. There on the top of the high piled wood the little girls made houses and played with their dolls. One of their innocent stories of a cave in the wood pile revealed a fraud perpetrated by a south end farmer, many cords short in his contract to the city.

West of Broadway was swamp, with a thick tangle of alders and other marsh growth, through which ran a tame sort of a creek where frogs held concerts. The boys who loved adventure cleaned out the snakes, but the crop of frogs seemingly grew no less though many found their way into the schoolrooms in coat pockets and were let loose to hop about on the girls' side. In this swamp the boys made robber dens in accordance with the fiction of the day.

There was a woman who had a home on the bank of the creek above Fifth-st. In a willow thicket below her house some girls innocently built a dam which blocked the water and drowned all the chickens. Of course, the engineering feat was laid to boys. I always liked that woman, but not well enough to give to her the names of the girls who played in that heaven of mud, water and pollywogs.

It seems to me there never was a schoolhouse with so many natural attractions for the boys and girls, but along with the years came the big ditch and swallowed the creek and the dump of the city buried the alders, willows and cattails. Mrs. Cool's garden, chickens and pump were outlawed. The old stone school was condemned in 1872 as a worn-out building and unsafe for the increasing numbers. While replacing it school was held in a long wooden shed built the length of the Third-st. side. The rooms were so exactly alike that small children became confused and had to be escorted to their places. The third school now stands on this location and enrolls more children than lived in all the city at the time the old stone school was built. Above the swamp where Dick built a robber's roost with a dime novel for a guide, his great-grandson is taught "how to play" and teeters on a board with a caretaker to see he does not fall off. The stone school that seemed built for eternity has become but a legend.

Rev. James Ballard, Schoolmaster

Many of the "gray locks" of today recall with great affection James Ballard, teacher, preacher, and orator, who came to Michigan from Vermont in 1838. He started to clear a farm in Paris township, but wrestling with log heaps and hunting stray cows was not congenial work for a college-bred man. He soon became an all around man in the community—schoolmaster, Baptist minister, temperance orator and at one time was a candidate for the legislature on a dry ticket, in a very wet district, receiving sixteen votes.

In the early fifties, he became the first principal of the two schools of the village, but not until 1858 did I make acquaintance with his hickory ruler as a pupil in the stone school on the west side.

In those days boys as well as steers were broken in with a gad. Mr. Ballard carried his goose-quill pen behind his ear and one day he caught me laughing at his efforts to keep his long black hair and the quill in place while he applied the ruler to Henry Goodsell. He called me out to hold the quill while he finished Henry and then his keen eyes twinkled while I got a bit of medicine myself.

One of his favorite punishments was to make an unruly boy sit on the girls' side of the room. I don't know what I did to arouse his wrath, but one day I was commanded to go sit with red-headed Emily Pettibone. Emily's father owned a fine piece of woods on West Bridge-st. in about the present locality of the St. James' church and she of the sunset locks was one of my best chums—as Mr. Ballard soon discovered, so the order was rescinded to bringing a pail of drinking water from Mrs. Cool's well.

For all the strict discipline he was friendly with the boys. The Armory at that time was on the third floor of the schoolhouse and on stormy days the older boys, with Mr. Ballard for umpire, put on boxing gloves and he played with the same pep with which he ruled.

One of the interesting things I recall of that school was the attendance for a short time of four Indian boys from Bass River. They spoke a dialect of Indian and French with very little English and it became my duty to work out on the blackboard their names in English. Some of the parents objected to this mixture in the schools and the boys were sent to the Pentwater reservation.

Mr. Ballard taught elocution with many gestures and much rolling of the r's. Every Friday afternoon was a period for recitations when he endeavored to fire the sapheads who mostly were too green to burn. He tried in vain to inspire one of these Indians with the fact that the "Ragged Rascal Ran" and rolled his r's all the time he was running, but finally gave up and told the boy to recite his own way. In perfect imitation of Mr. Ballard's most impressive gestures the Indian gravely proclaimed, "The d— thief run like h—," and the principal was the first to shout his approval.

For a long time Mr. Ballard filled the pulpit of the little church at Steele's landing, now Lamont. The country was being rapidly settled with the best of eastern people, almost to a man American born. There were few papers to spread the news and the preacher's two-hour talk was a fine treat, for he went to them with head and heart full of the great events of the day.

Those were abolition days and there was an underground route for the black man that touched Steele's landing on the way from the south to Canada.

One Sunday afternoon I was at the landing with my canoe and was somewhat overawed when the preacher asked to go home with me. Farmers usually gave him a lift part of the way or the steamboat came along. He made himself a cushion of wild grape vine in the bow with a piece of driftwood for a back, talked of the river and sang, not the chantys of the river man, but Scotch and Irish melodies, until he fell asleep. And I knew that my schoolmaster was at heart only a boy after all.

The West Side Meeting House

This meeting house fronted Bridge-st. near the west end of the bridge. It was there when I came to town and I had no right to find fault with it, but some way it got on my nerves. There was nothing about it that appealed to a boy of my build, especially on bright Sunday mornings.

Painted Venetian red outside and smoke-tanned to a faded olive inside, the windows were of seven by nine glass. One of the deacons was known as "Old Seven By Nine."

The seats were clear stuff pine in straight lines. There was no place for a shoulder blade or an angle where a fellow could rest his conscience. Sometimes in summer, clouds of fish flies swarmed outside and a few thousands were snared in the cobwebs that ornamented the interior. There were two large box stoves which the boys were supposed to feed on cold days.

There was nothing that would drive a boy to the woods much quicker than the thought of bucking up wood on Sunday morning. If the people who made up the congregation had not been the best Christians in the world the ministers who came there to preach would have died of homesickness.

Grand Rapids at this time was blessed with good singers, men and women, and the church had its share of them. If the preacher found only misery and judgment in his text the choir assisted the congregation to something like happiness and content. There was no organ and the belief that the fiddle was a part of Satan's outfit had a strong hold on this west side meeting house.

Henry Stone was an officer and member of the church. He was also a fine musician and being of Revolutionary stock he made no attempt to smother the fife and drum. He also played the fiddle and rosined his bow for the hymns, pitching the tune for the members of the choir. It was one Easter morning and all the country and town folk assembled for service, when, for the first time in the history of that meeting house, the clear notes of a fife penetrated the peaceful atmosphere.

Henry Stone certainly made everyone sit up and take notice. It was like a warning that old Nick himself had arrived. Some of the deacons blew their noses loudly, others wiped their unbelieving spectacles. Old Mrs. Weinberger, whom the boys rather fittingly called "Mrs. Vinegar," grabbed at her brood of four and marched out.

The following Sunday Henry came in with his fiddle and the congregation gave a good imitation of bumble-bees about to swarm. Some of those dear old people continued to buzz until a traveling peddler came along and sold the church a melodian that groaned as if it was full of pain and green apples.

Thanks to Henry Stone the church began to hold some interest for the boys. Also the real musical education of the west side boomed that summer. At a corner bench in dad's shop, now moved to the west side, the boys worked busily on cane fish poles. Cut into lengths between joints, they made good fifes and the boys also acquired considerable skill in making corn-stalk fiddles. A large crop of these musical instruments were produced and some of them are today family keepsakes of the old west side people. And through it all Henry, unafraid, marched with his fife at the head of the Fourth of July parade.

With the City Firemen

One afternoon in 1857, I occupied a reserved seat on the top of a house on Monroe street along with some forty odd boys and girls and saw twenty-five business places destroyed by fire. The fire started in a drug store on Monroe between Waterloo and Ottawa-sts.

There were three fire companies at that time and Number One and Number Two were in the crater, while Number Three was working to save surrounding property. It looked from my position as if all the people of the town were helping; throwing glass and china from upper windows and lugging feather beds down stairways.

From one of the stores many large boxes of dry paints were carried into the street. Every store kept whisky in those days: none of them drinking water. As a result the male population, thirsty and hard pressed by the flames, got a little dizzy and began tumbling into the paint boxes. Yellows and greens and purple began to blend with the blue and gray of smoke and ashes. If any of you have a desire to know how funny a man really can look, fill his inside with fire water and his outside with the colors of the rainbow.

Were it not that the wind-driven fire brands threatened the entire town it would have been the most successful carnival the people ever put on the street.

From a doctor's office some fellows salvaged a pickling cask. It tipped into the gutter and scattered the contents and an Indian with a scalping knife could not have stampeded a crowd more quickly.

Number One and Number Two fire companies became

badly demoralized by evening. Overcome by spirits and crusted with color they disappeared from the scene of conflagration. Number Three saved the town by working until daylight next morning. The women keeping them going by carrying coffee and sandwiches. The following Sunday every church in town was given a sermon on temperance.

As a reward of merit to Number Three company for keeping sober, the women of the town expressed their appreciation by the gift of a beautiful satin banner, which is now among the treasures of the Kent Scientific Museum.

This fire had all the thrills of a great battle. It was the fireside story of the year and while it distressed many people for a long time, now that the paint is washed off they can smile, even at the foreman of the company, who, lying on his back in a box of red paint, waived his brass trumpet vaguely and shouted: "Play away, Number Two."

Firemen of the Fifties

Fire fighting is an inherited trait. Every boy gloried in his father on parade. When the town had three fire companies there was an auxiliary force of small sons following up each one. The writer was a trailer of Number Three and feels that he would not be loyal to the memory of that west side auxiliary if he had no word for their achievements.

In the fall, "when the frost was on the vine" and fires about the stumps on vacant lots gave enchantment to the night, war dances were staged. They were the only dances many of the boys could have, for their parents belonged to a church which prohibited such exercise.

The commons on Stocking-av. was a great congregating place, stumps being plentiful. Nearby there lived a good old colored mammy whose gifts as a fortune teller had brought her fame and some wealth.

In the shuffling of cards she always found "a handsome young gentleman sure after you, my dear lady. You keep track of your steps and he sure done catch up with you."

Moreover, she found good fortune for the moderate sum of

twenty-five cents. Between seasons she hung out a sign, "Goin' out washun dun here."

The madam's house, a two-story structure, had so many lean-tos built on that a boy could jump from the rain barrel to the roof of the first and then by series of angles and climbs reach the peak of the main roof out of which came the stovepipe from the lower floor.

At that date there were not many colored people here, but they had a little church and every once in a while had a social to raise funds for repairing the shingles.

One evening the social was at the madam's and every colored person in town was in attendance. They were just about eating up the results of the shingle collection when Number Three fire auxiliary, playing about a blazing stump on the commons, discovered madam's chimney on fire—a roaring torch in the gloom of a cloudy night. In breathless haste the boys formed a bucket brigade and, shinning up the various roofs, the most daring hero reached the peak and turned the first and only bucket of water into the red-hot pipe.

One must have a fireman's experience to know what happened to the social below; a bang like a thunderbolt, soot, ashes, fire and steam. By the time the folks had the cinders out of their eyes and the fear of the Lord out of their hearts the firemen sensed they had stirred up something.

Faster running was done in getting away from that fire than was ever done in getting to another, and all that fall and winter the sons of Number Three held their war dances in another place on the west side.

My Fire Service Before the Civil War

When about fourteen years old I became interested in Number Three fire company. My father was a member and it was every boy's ambition to run with the engine.

No salaries were paid; in fact, one had to pay fifty cents annual dues and fifty cents fine for missing a fire or monthly meeting. I was assigned the duty of bearing the torch, a brass globe that held about a quart of fish oil on the end of a four-foot staff. I must be first man at the engine house and with

OF GRAND RAPIDS

the torch run ahead of the machine to light the road to the fire. Once there and the machine set, I must go with the pipeman and light the way into stairways and other dark places. It certainly was a life of adventure.

It was my start in public affairs and caused many sleepless hours, with no pay, in return. I rather think those men and boys would have felt insulted if pay had been offered them.

Mother made me a red shirt and embroidered in silk on the front a figure three. Every time I carried the torch mother had to wash the fish oil out of my clothes. That was one of the penalties she paid for the glory of having a fireman in the family.

I had the trade pretty well learned by the beginning of the Civil war and when the various war organizations absorbed nearly every able-bodied man in Number Three company it became necessary to make up a new hose company.

I was elected foreman with a silver plated trumpet as a badge of authority. I had reached the top round of the ladder. Boys had attained a commercial value then and the common council announced they would pay five dollars each at the end of a year's service.

When the year ended the city clerk, Mr. Doubleday, sent each one of the company an order for five dollars, but there was no money in the treasury. Then John W. Squires, the miller, said he would give us a two hundred-pound barrel of flour for each order.

I went to his mill, built of river stone on the river's east bank, not far south of the bridge, and took my flour home in my canoe to save expense. It was the proudest moment of my fire fighting life when I rolled that barrel of flour into mother's kitchen. My father was in the army and a whole barrel of flour at one time was cause for a jubilee. I was one of twenty boys who made their mothers happy that day.

I am quite certain that this was the first pay ever given volunteer firemen in this city.

Hose company Number Three became a west side institution. The members were from the best families and were a live bunch. Nearly all men of military age being in the first call for war, the sons began to keep the home fires burning. They found time to buck up wood for the kitchen stoves and play man of the house. They had a regular drill night at the Armory, where soldiers were made, and a weekly social dance at the engine house, with an invitation list and printed program. Tickets were fifty cents and there was a company fund to meet expenses.

From this training, the early days of 1862 called them to army service almost to a man and they stepped naturally into the ranks. And though this is not a war story just let me state, that of the eighteen boys who marched away from Number Three fire company, fourteen sleep in the ground of the sunny South.

Experience of a Volunteer Fireman

There was no small responsibility attached to the job of being a fireman in the early days of the town. Most of the buildings were of wood and lumber yards were numerous. All the fuel was wood. Fish oil, tallow candles and camphene furnished light. It took very little to start a fire and there was always plenty of combustible material for it to feed upon. So a fireman's responsibilities were never far from mind.

One never heard, in those days, of nervous prostration. When the bottom fell out of the pork barrel a man did not stop to wash his face in the brine. In all their hard times those firemen kept their shirts, belts and caps on the parlor table ready for instant use and while not nervous they gained a fire instinct that many a time had them on the run for the engine house before the alarm sounded.

During my ten years' experience in fire fighting I was often dressed before the alarm box sounded, and once stood in the street, holding my horse by the bridle, until a glow on the sky gave me my direction.

The night the Eagle hotel burned, in the early eighties, my gray saddle mare kicked her way out of the stable and was at the fire a mile away before any of the firemen were there. No one knew how long it had been smoldering, but the entire building came down with a crash before half of the department was at hand. Often when I became assistant chief men came to me with their resignations and the excuse was, "It's getting on my nerves. I am out before the alarm and I am going to quit."

When David Caswell was foreman of Number Three there was one volunteer, a leading citizen and daring fire fighter, who often came to him predicting fires but not their localities. So accurate were his predictions that he and other members of the company sometimes slept in the engine house waiting the call.

Finally this man told Mr. Caswell there was going to be a fire longer than a street and threatening the entire town, and for two nights men slept on the floor of the engine house and those living near by, in most of their clothing. This was a long time before the invention of electric fire alarms and when there were no night police.

When the call finally came, the woodenware factory belonging to Mr. Caswell just at the east end of the bridge, was all ablaze. With a rush Number Three machine and crew ran under cover of the bridge, but so rapidly did the fire spread over the bridge that men hauling the engine were scorched and those following jumped into the river to save their lives. They got their engine safely to the east side, but the bridge was completely destroyed and they had to load the engine on a scow above the dam to get it back to the engine house on the west side.

The man I referred to as predicting this fire became for a time an object of gossip and suspicion, but loved and trusted by his companions, he did not leave the company—simply ceased to give his warnings because sensitive to the attention being drawn to himself.

One of the most daring feats ever performed by a fireman was that of Tom Bedell of Number Two company at an early morning blaze that destroyed the Bissell Carpet Sweeper plant. Trapped on the upper floor he dropped from a fifth story window to the window ledges below, making five successful drops and catching each ledge until he reached the ground practically unharmed.

THE YESTERDAYS

The Volunteer Firemen of Early Days

The first fire engine in Grand Rapids was the hand work of one of its own citizens, William Peaslee. It was made in 1846 and it cost sixty dollars to build an engine house to shelter it.

The engine was of the tub pattern. The tub, thirty by sixty inches and fifteen inches deep, was set on dead axles and on wheels thirty inches high. The water must be first dipped in by buckets, often from the river. Once a red-fin mullet choked the pump and before they got the fish out the building was a total loss to the insurance company.

In service the pioneer engine was pushed close to the fire, the water turned in with buckets and pumped out by four men, two on either side.

The drawback to this engine was the reluctance of men and women to line up from the river to the fire and pass full buckets one way and empty ones the other. Everybody wanted to be near the fire and see the engine squirt. To help out this laudable ambition cisterns were built at some street intersections. These could be filled by roof water on rainy days. The public cisterns were helped out by wells and dwelling house cisterns. There existed a belief in scientific minds that soft rain water pumped easier than hard spring water and many housewives found dry cisterns on wash-day.

Finally some public spirited men passed the hat and with six hundred and seventy-five dollars secured from the same builder a larger engine that required sixteen men to pump and would throw five barrels of water a minute over the roof of a two-story building.

This engine was stored in the schoolhouse on Prospect hill. The town then had two fire engines—one to throw a short, the other a long distance, much like the houses in Shantytown that had two holes in the outside door, one large to let the old cat in, the other small for the kitten.

Many of the men who manned the second engine, living a long distance away, were wind-broken before they reached the hilltop and seldom had a fair show at a fire.

The new engine had a suction to fill the tub when the fire

happened to be near a cistern or the river, but as the department had but two hundred and fifty feet of hose the bucket brigade was not disbanded.

The hose, made of heavy sole leather riveted with copper, cost a lot of money. Greasing it twice a year with neat's-foot oil took much of the romance out of the lives of the hose company.

The men who served on these engines were unpaid volunteers. Every live man wanted to be identified with the fire department and the town was blessed with live men. There were a scattering few known as "basswood hams" who did not run with the machine when the fire bell rang.

While no one drew pay these firemen were fined fifty cents if absent from a fire. In his uniform of red shirt, brickbat hat, and patent leather belt, the fireman was the admiration of the fair sex. Often when the alarm came it took so long for a man to run home, slip on his red shirt and his belt—for how else could he keep his trousers up—that by the time he arrived the fire had burned itself out. The foreman with his brass trumpet was the envy of the boys.

Once a week the firemen had a dance, to which only those in good standing were admitted. Tickets at fifty cents paid for music and invitations. Supper was extra. If a fellow came in with a liquor breath they threw him out so hard he never came back.

These were little sprouts leading to the growth of our department as we have it today. Then, if the department arrived at the fire in thirty minutes it had made good time. Today, if not there in thirty seconds it is investigated. If our present fire marshal was seen running down Monroe-av. with a brass trumpet looking for his fire company he would land in the state hospital at Kalamazoo.

Old Volunteer Firemen

Often in dodging traffic on Campau Square the writer runs head on to Warren C. Weatherly, who fifty odd years ago was foreman in a rival volunteer fire company. He boosted with all his might for Number One. I pegged for Number Three.

THE YESTERDAYS

At the present time fire fighting is a profession calling for bravery and the best physical strength. The men are paid for their service and sometimes earn a great deal more than they receive. In the early days of the town men had the same qualifications but were not on the pay roll. Fire fighting was a public duty. Civic pride and the saving of life and property were the incentives; to many men it was a time of adventure. The men equipped themselves often to the extent of paying for their fire fighting apparatus.

When the first Lagrave-st. fire station, called Number One, was built, Mr. Weatherly, then in the service, selected and organized the men who made up the company. With rare good judgment he selected from the volunteer force Henry Lemoine, afterward chief of the department, giving his entire life to the service, and Solon Baxter, a Civil war cavalryman who for many years, as assistant chief, gave exhibitions of daring horsemanship through the busy streets. Then there was Henry Carr, the son of a noted Civil war officer. He left the fire company to become a city librarian and is now at Scranton, Pa., one of the noted men of the country in that profession. Mr. Weatherly, himself, as a sanitary engineer and builder, is well known in every city of the state.

The men named indicate the caliber of Number One company. Their energies were directed to building up the fire fighting force that the city required. One of New York's famous regiments in the Civil war were all volunteer firemen and so powerful were they in the life of the community that city councils began to use them as a political body.

The firemen in Grand Rapids could not be handled in that way. Each ward alderman worked for his own interest, so everything in the way of better equipment came slowly and often at the expense of the firemen themselves.

Grand Rapids was a mill town and fires were frequent and often fierce because it took so long to get in the alarm. At night the glow on the sky was all the guide we had. To be the first to get a stream of water on the fire was a company's ambition and Foreman Weatherly of Number One began ways to secure quick alarms for his men. There was one all-night police station where the Grand Rapids Savings bank is now located and there the calls were first reported. Mr. Weatherly studied out a plan to connect the Lagrave-st. fire station with the police station by wire and scoop the other companies. The cost of the material would be eighty dollars. He petitioned the city council to pay half this cost. He would contribute the labor and if the scheme was a failure he agreed to stand all the expense.

He arranged an electrical alarm, a twelve-inch gong alongside a twelve-inch clock dial, which in turning would make a contact with round brass head nails. From the nails a wire was to lead to the home and bedside of each member of the company. The police would receive the alarm and then swing the dial until the round of numbers had been called.

The plan was a success and the Lagrave-st. boys beat the other companies to the fires, so these petitioned for the same favor, but the council after weeks of debate decided to put in six Gamewell fire alarm boxes in different sections of the city.

The firemen, disgusted with the slow going aldermen, quietly began a game of their own, and through legislative action placed the department in the control of a commission that served the entire city and in time gave Grand Rapids the best fire department in the country. From Mr. Weatherly's beginnings, the savings in insurance alone to the property owners, has been many times the cost and maintenance of the department.

The surviving members of the old volunteer companies will always recall with gratitude the women of their day who so loyally aided them in times of unusual stress. The mill and lumber yard fires were often fierce affairs and no matter how bad the sleet or snow or darkness, some good woman was sure to come with hot coffee, sandwiches or doughnuts. Mrs. Wilder D. Foster, Mrs. Charlotte Richards, Mrs. James D. Robinson and my own dear mother, come to mind as some of the good angels of the day, though there were many others who deserve equal credit.

THE YESTERDAYS

Number Three's Engine House

The membership of Number Three fire company included all the real live men of the community, men of all trades and professions. At this date it would be difficult for me to recall all the names of those leaders of thought and action, many of whom in the days of the Civil war won rank and title.

Beginning in 1859 and finishing in 1860, without public aid, they secured the lot and built the engine house on Scribner-st., for many years past occupied by the West Side Ladies' Literary club.

Most of the labor on this building was done after six o'clock on summer evenings. Men who had put in ten hours on day jobs hurried to the engine house and worked until darkness drove them home. Often the wife with a baby on one arm and a basket on the other met her husband and they had supper at the building so that no minute of daylight would be lost. In those days the town owed no man a living. Every man felt he owed the community all that he could give for its advancement.

As the front of our engine house took shape, pillars of Grand Rapids marble quarried in the Hovey plaster mines were cut and polished for either side of the door. These were the only parts of the building that proved not durable. Doors and window frames of elaborate design were made by hand. Fine stained glass windows were put in. The glass came from Chicago and was very carefully spread out and studied over before being leaded into place. The color effects were highly satisfactory in the glow of the afternoon sun.

An artist lettered the wall in gold leaf "Alpha and Omega." Not many of the men knew what this meant, but were careful not to expose their ignorance.

The opening night was the great event of the year. All the town was there. There was the best of music by a score of fiddlers and dancing kept up until daylight. Some of the good church people danced and later were summoned before the church dignitaries for discipline.

Never again until the great homecoming dinner served on Pearl-st. bridge at the close of the Civil war were so many beautiful ladies at one gathering. In an improvised bower in the rear of the lower floor were two barrels of lemonade; the one for men had a stick in it. At midnight a fine supper was served. All the table silverware on the west side was there and although a colored string was tied to each piece it took the balance of the summer to separate and return it to the rightful owners.

Not until Civil war days was the engine house dropped from the social calendar. Occasionally the rival companies or a revengeful, rejected guest started a fire in a slab pile or shingle mill just to break up the festivities. The firemen always kept their fire shirts and rough pants ready for emergency and if an alarm came in there was a wild scramble to get out of party clothes and on the run with the hand engine and hose reel.

Fire Company Number Three Visits Muskegon

Here is a word of greeting to old-time firemen of the "Mill Town" on the lake, who in sawdust days of the seventies sometimes called on Grand Rapids for assistance.

The Muskegon firemen, under Chief Frank Jiroch, were as efficient as America produced, but when fire started in the mills or lumber yards it had the aid of the winds from the lake and spread with such rapidity that often every effort had to be devoted to saving life while the fire sometimes spread from mills and lumber to the entire business and residence section.

Grand Rapids always made a quick response to these calls from neighboring towns and they were numerous. For convenience, a flat car was kept by the G. R. & I. railroad at a landing platform near its west Bridge-st. station.

One wild night in September, 1874, when the wind was blowing a forty-mile gale, Number Three company was called to load a steamer and hose cart for Muskegon. The western sky was aglow and the stars were playing hide and seek with the fast flying clouds, when we cleared the junction—now Fuller station—and headed toward Nunica, where we switched for Muskegon.

THE YESTERDAYS

I was the foreman of Number Three and felt a certain responsibility for the safe conduct of the expedition, but had to exercise most of it in hanging to the hose cart. It seemed the way that flat car jumped about that George Elliot, the engineer of the locomotive, and James Bessey, his fireman, had taken cross lots and were dodging stumps and cattle.

Elliot had one hand on the lever and the other pulling the whistle cord, while Bessey kept a line of wood going into the furnace and a swirl of coals and sparks rolling from the stack over the firemen, who were clinging to the steamer and cart wheels.

We were making a mile a minute and if we had struck one of the cows that were running at large, the man in the moon would have had cream in his morning coffee.

I tried to beg for more caution but was kept too busy spitting cinders. Then I saw Jim Bessey, who had served in my company during the Civil war, grinning at me over the top of the wood pile on the tender and my confidence returned.

The track has been cleared at both switching points and we arrived in Muskegon about one a. m. A nervy driver with a pair of horses ran the company down a long avenue of burning wreckage. Even the roadway of plank and sawdust was ablaze in places. But we had to make it in order to reach the slip at the lake and get water. The fire had spread all along the lake front. The Muskegon firemen had lost line after line of hose, part of their apparatus, and with burned hands and blistered faces were still putting up a heroic fight. We were soon putting up about as desperate a battle ourselves, for mills, lumber yards, business places and homes were being wiped out over at least fifteen blocks.

Into this furnace where we were working, came a man who seemed to be warped out of shape by the heat. He pleaded, "For God's Sake, save my lot. My house is gone, my shop, my barn—everything is gone but the lot. Save that!"

There have been times when my head has been so thick that I have been slow in catching on. I was somewhat dazed and not until the fire was checked did I realize that his lot was a long-time accumulation of slabs and sawdust resting on a foundation of lily pads and cattails. We heeded his prayer and flooded the place before we withdrew for another location. In after years I tried in vain to locate that lot, but when I see the pleasant streets, the parks and fine buildings of today, I rejoice that Number Three was able at least to save the ground on which they stand.

We worked steadily on that fire until late the following afternoon. Citizens kept us supplied with coffee and sandwiches until we were ready to return to Grand Rapids. Then we were given a dinner at the best hotel and the mayor was on hand to thank us. I am sorry that I cannot recall the name of the mayor, for his expressions of gratitude repaid the Grand Rapids firemen many times and made us feel we had been serving our own home folks.

When our outfit was again loaded upon the flat car we made George Elliot promise to stick to the rails on the way home. Then all lay down to sleep on the floor of the old flat car.

General I. C. Smith's "Pony"

In the seventies large droves of saddle horses were shipped from the western plains to eastern markets. Many of these animals had been used by the cattle herdsmen and buffalo hunters and not a few in army service against the Indians. Many horses were branded with the mark "U. S." and saddle scars were frequent and denoted training.

From one of these droves General Smith selected for the fire department, of which he was chief, a horse that responded to the name Pony. Besides a ranch brand he bore several scars, but none that disfigured him. He had a dark, almost black, silken coat, three white ankles and a three point white star on his forehead.

General Smith, noted in the Civil war cavalry for his horsemanship, had also seen service on the cattle ranges of Kansas and Colorado and had had experience as a buffalo hunter. At first sight he bought the Pony, but was also attracted to a bay horse, free from blemish except for the faint brand U. S. Baby was his name and he was a garrison horse—a woman's pet, excitable but kind and a perfect saddler.

THE YESTERDAYS

The salesman was reluctant to part with him, but finally did so because the general was taking Pony. These two saddle horses cost the city about two hundred dollars and because other horses of this lot were sold at fifty dollars or less the grumbling of some of the city fathers was long and loud.

Baby was kept as an extra supply horse and we often rode him to keep him in trim, but the general found in Pony his ideal for speed, gait and style. About this time the buffalo robe was the popular covering used by farmers, city drivers or livery stables, in wagons or sleighs, and cold weather had no sooner set in than the general learned that Pony's scars had come from horn or hoof and gone in deeper than the hide.

The odor of the robes, even in a stable, gave the horse a nervous chill and the sight of one threw him into a panic. While running for a fire on North Canal street one day the general cut close in the rear of a farm wagon. Pony made a lunge to the side that landed his rider full length on his back —fortunately on the buffalo robe in the wagon body.

Three times that winter the general was unhorsed by Pony jumping from under him and finally he made a headlong slide on the street car track, breaking the general's ankle and laying him up several weeks.

Jimmie Howell, the supply driver, took so many tumbles that no count was kept of them. When the general left the fire service no one was found to ride the Pony and deprived of his exercise he soon had to be retired.

Baby, the supply horse, had evidently been an army post pet, probably stolen by some horse thief, for it would seem that no soldier would ever have parted with so lovable and intelligent an animal. Neither whip nor spur was ever used on him and the call of a bugle or sound of a band put him on parade in an instant.

In those days there were a great many fine saddle horses, several of the police officers were well mounted and riding was a popular diversion with both men and women.

Every parade brought out the best the city had and the fire department was always a prominent feature. On two or three Fourth of July's the town staged what was very properly termed Horribles. In 1878 an added feature of the parade was an Indian pageant managed by General Smith, who impersonated Sitting Bull. I loaned my horse Fly to a friend and all rigged up as Lone Star was mounted on Baby. We were the real thing; even our families did not recognize us—war paint, feather bonnets and moccasins, riding bare back and our only saddle equipment a mouth strap.

The streets were jammed with people and when the parade started the profanity of the Horribles, the whooping of Indians and waving of war bonnets went all right with the average horse, but was too much for the nerves of Pony and the Baby. Sitting Bull left very hurriedly for the east and after a rest somewhere in the vicinity of Fisk lake returned to his home on Lagrave street after dark.

Baby headed up Canal street, as wild a horse as ever carried an Indian. How the people ever saved themselves I do not know, except that the horse jumped over those he could not dodge. Wet with perspiration he became slippery as an eel and trained to rein by a touch on the neck the mouth strap would not halt him. When I tried to hold him I slipped up near his ears, so when nearing the city pumping station and a clear plot of lawn, I leaned far over and gripped his nostrils, choking off his wind. We keeled head over heels on the grass and some time later sneaked through back streets to Number Four engine house for a rubdown.

There was one Sitting Bull and one Lone Star, one Pony and one Baby, who never appeared in another Indian celebration.

My Gray Fire Horse

From 1864, when Grand Rapids fire teams were only volunteer affairs, social organizations, kept going mainly by entertainments and private gifts, changes came rapidly until the early seventies when by a combination of events Gen. I. C. Smith—new to fire work—was made chief of the department as an organizer and I became his assistant because of my fire service.

To facilitate the work, Gen. Smith and I procured saddle horses which became as well known to the public as were any of the men of the town. They raced neck and neck to many a fire, the general's dark bay with three white feet and my gray mare, and they dearly loved the cheers of the people along the way. Many folks remember my Fly and have asked me to tell something about her.

Julius Berkey bought this thoroughbred Kentucky colt for his daughter's use. She was well broken to the saddle but too high strung for city life, so Mr. Berkey offered her to me for two hundred and twenty-five dollars just what he gave for her in Kentucky. The city paid me a salary of six hundred dollars per annum but did not figure on horse feed. My first year's pay went for equipment, which included saddle, bridle, a buggy, harness and blankets, and I used the outfit as I pleased in my private business also.

The first man to mount Fly was going to show me how to ride, but she took the bits between her teeth and carried him about five blocks, dumped him headlong over a garden fence and returned to the stable.

During my army life I acquired the habit of talking to my horse and from the first meeting with the gray I fell naturally into the old lingo. She seemed to understand and answered with her ears. Sugar always brought a delighted whinny and I seldom failed to share at least the core of my apple.

One unfortunate office boy, Frank Widoe by name, will never forget the punishment she administered for tantalizing her with an apple. When tired of begging for a bite she gathered his coat collar in her teeth and shook him until his cries brought the entire office force to the rescue.

I lived several blocks from the engine house and had a private alarm connection in my sleeping room. It took but a moment to reach the stable, throw on the saddle and be on the street. Frequently my wife counted the box number and called it as I dashed past, but at night the glow on the sky was usually a sufficient guide and the mare covered ground while I finished dressing. She seemed always first to hear the bell and if I was slow in responding nearly kicked the stable down. Once she made her way out a side door and departed over a back lot fence, reporting for duty while I went on foot.

One stormy winter night she shied from under me at the corner of Third and Turner so suddenly that I sat behind her ears for half a block. Returning later from the fire she danced to the sidewalk at the same place. I dismounted to investigate and found a drunken man stretched full length, his clothing frozen stiff in the mud.

Number Three men came with lanterns, chopped him loose and took him to the station to thaw out.

One other bitterly cold night when the wind whirled the snow up Canal-st., crowds of men sought the shelter of nearby store doorways to watch the fire in a hardware store. I dismounted, as was my custom, leaving the horse to care for herself. With open mouth she charged a doorway shelter and held the fort until one of the steamer drivers came to cover her with a blanket.

The wind gave the firemen on the upper floor a hard fight and a little later when I was half way up a ladder I heard the crowd on the street cheering and looking down saw Fly with her front feet on the third round of the ladder trying to follow me.

Once we were called to the Nelson-Matter furniture factory on Lyon-st. A fire in the basement filled the main floor and machine room with dense smoke. Firemen had no gas masks in those days and I was struggling through the stifling air, feeling my way between machines and trying to locate the source of the trouble. I heard steps behind me and thought the pipemen were coming with a line of hose until the snort of my horse came full in my face. I made what haste I could to get her out, but we were both nearly suffocated.

For four years Fly never lost a run. Then came a fierce factory fire on upper Canal-st. and in an attempt to follow me she was caught on a street with fire on either side and before I could mount and get away was seriously burned on face and neck. For six weeks I rode a little terror named Baby that the department had purchased as an extra for the chief.

THE YESTERDAYS OF GRAND RAPIDS

Long after I had my fill of fire fighting and had retired from service the little mare made the most of every opportunity to keep in the game.

One night, excited by the glare on the sky, she kicked the stable door open and was about the first on the scene at the burning of the Eagle hotel. I followed with the saddle on my shoulders and the old comrades gave us a hearty cheer. Twice the mare took the bits in her teeth and ran away to fires when my wife was driving, and one evening when my young daughter was in the saddle she made a record run to the south end of town.

When James G. Blaine came to the city for a great political gathering I loaned Fly to a friend and rode the supply horse. We paraded down from the old Grand Trunk station. Fly loved to play in the water and while passing a watering trough at Coldbrook crossing she ran her nose to the bottom of the tank, blew water in every direction and then jumping from under my friend left him lying in the mud while she made full speed for the head of the column.

During old age Fly was retired to the farm of George Stage, on the Alpine town line north and was finally wrapped in her blankets and buried under a clump of maples.

I'll say for my little gray horse, she was one of the most faithful scouts the fire department ever had.

0 016 099 499 A